THE EVERYTHING

WEDDING VOWS BOOK

Revised and Expanded
Second Edition

Anything and everything you could possibly say at the altar—and then some

Janet Anastasio and Michelle Bevilacqua

with Leah Furman and Elina Furman

Adams Media Corporation
Avon, Massachusetts

An Everything® Series Book.
Everything® is a registered trademark
of Adams Media Corporation.

Published by Adams Media Corporation
57 Littlefield Street, Avon, MA 02322. U.S.A.
www.adamsmedia.com

ISBN: 1-58062-455-3

Printed in Canada.

J I H G F E D C

Library of Congress Cataloging-in-Publication Data
available from publisher upon request.

This publication is designed to provide accurate and authoritative
information with regard to the subject matter covered. It is sold with
the understanding that the publisher is not engaged in rendering
legal, accounting, or other professional advice. If legal advice or other
expert assistance is required, the services of a competent professional
person should be sought.
— From a *Declaration of Principles* jointly adopted by a Committee
of the American Bar Association and a Committee of Publishers
and Associations

Many of the designations used by manufacturers and sellers to dis-
tinguish their products are claimed as trademarks. Where those designations have appeared in this book and Adams Media was aware
of a trademark claim, the designations have been printed in initial
capital letters.

Illustrations by Barry Littmann and Kathie Kelleher.

*This book is available at quantity discounts for bulk purchases.
For information, call 1-800-872-5627.*

Contents

CHAPTER ONE

Off to a Good Start

*P*lanning a wedding can be a hard and thankless task, but writing your vows shouldn't have to be. Here's where you and your loved one get to look deep into each other's eyes and work together for the good of the ceremony and your future as a married couple. The time you spend in crafting your words of love and devotion is all about you. Forget about the seating arrangements, the bridesmaids' dresses, and the color schemes. No need to worry about the caterer, the photographer, and all the money you'll have to spend. As one of the best things in life, wedding vows are absolutely free.

They are also yours to do with as you please. Choosing to write your own vows shows that you are an independent and adventurous couple, a pairing of two free spirits unafraid to tell the world how you truly feel about one another. It takes a brave person to compose personalized vows and bare his or her soul before a room full of people. This isn't about falling back on thin-worn clichés or trying to do it the way it's done in the movies. Expressing your feelings your way is like telling the truth—much more interesting and a hundred times more touching than any work of fiction.

Important note: Before you get too far along in the process of creating a personalized vow—and before you get too attached to what you've created—check with your ceremony officiant for guidelines on how to proceed. Different traditions take different approaches on the question of what should or should not be said at the altar. Some religions can be strict about what vows must be said, while others are more flexible.

Be sure to resolve all important issues along these lines early on in the process. You don't want to have to make changes at the last minute!

If you are considering developing your own wedding vows, it's probably because you want to formalize your commitment with something unique, something that is specific to your relationship or situation. You want the words you say on the big day to mean something that is truly meaningful to both of you. This is not to say that the traditional vows aren't special or meaningful—but vows you create yourself will be more personalized.

The Basics

Perhaps the best way to get you off on the right foot is to revisit the dictionary definition of the word *vow*. According to good ol' Merriam-Webster, a vow is "a solemn promise or assertion . . . by which a person is bound to an act, service, or condition."

On the basis of this definition alone, the decision to write your own vows or adapt the traditional vows makes perfect sense. After all, if you're binding yourself for life, shouldn't you have a say in what it is that you're binding yourself to? Not so long ago, wives were bound to obey their husbands. But thanks to the vociferous protestations of brides everywhere, grooms can kiss those days good-bye. For hundreds of years, however, no one even gave that old "obey" clause so much as a second's thought. Fixed and impermeable, traditions were not meant to be broken. It's only in recent times that people have begun to stray from the fray and blaze their own trails.

Today, when it comes to exchanging vows, almost anything goes. Mixing and matching traditional vows, incorporating lines of poetry, or writing it all yourself are all acceptable. The solemn nature of the vows, however, has not changed. You're still making a pledge before all and sundry, so keep this in mind as you write: What exactly are you promising your betrothed?

Custom-Made Ceremony

At most wedding ceremonies, the officiant usually does most of the talking. But did you know that you may be able to put the words right into this master of ceremonies' mouth? Nowadays, everything from the "we are gathered here today" greeting passage to the "with this ring, I thee wed" ring exchange to the "I now pronounce you husband and wife" closing is up for negotiation.

Although this will probably mean more work for you and your intended, redesigning your wedding ceremony can make all the difference in the world. If you're going for an unconventional affair, you might not want to hear the familiar standards recited at your wedding. Certainly, if you're the type who usually opts out of the "boring" ceremony and heads straight for the reception, then this alternative wedding scenario is the one for you. As always, be sure to check with your officiant before forging ahead with Project: Ceremony Perestroika. You'll find more information on personalizing your ceremony in Chapter 4, "A Ceremony All Your Own."

Fear No More

If you're feeling a bit nervous, don't worry. Your apprehension has been faced by everyone who has ever attempted the daunting task of writing his or her own vows. But as you consider all that's at stake during this moment at the altar, try to forget about the guests, the in-laws, and your officiant. Although they'll be there to hear you speak your vows, this part of the ceremony is strictly between you and your fiancé. Listen to your heart, and the words will follow.

If you're thinking that this bit of advice is easier to give than to follow, you're probably not in the vow-writing mood at the moment. To get into the spirit of the process, we recommend the following visualization exercise: Imagine that you're alone in a log cabin with your partner. Bright sunlight is streaming in through the expansive windows. You're exactly where you want to be, you can stay here forever, and, best of all, both of you know it. There isn't a soul for miles around, the only thing you can see are your fiancé's eyes, full of love and compassion, and the only thing you can hear is the beating of your heart as you tell your true love how you really feel. This is the state of mind you will need to enter if your wish is to write truly meaningful vows.

Place and Time Springboards

You should feel free to incorporate the location of your wedding into your vows. For instance, if you and your fiancé are planning a ceremony on or near the water, perhaps on a sailboat or at a seaside resort, you might want to incorporate this in some way in your wedding vows. (In Chapter 5, you will find several sets of verses that can be adapted to weddings on or near the water, as well as dozens of other verses that may be appropriate for your situation.) You may decide the very best way to emphasize the importance of the location to you and your guests is for you and your partner to compose an original poem of your own.

The time of year might also bear mentioning in your vows. Why, for instance, did you decide on an April wedding? Could it have something to do with the renaissance that is the

Help for the Slightly Insecure

It's not every day that we dig down to the bottom of our hearts to come up with the perfect expression of our love. And with good reason: Saying exactly what we feel can be extremely frightening. Talk about your vulnerable situations. On the one hand, you want to find just the right words to express the depth of your emotion; on the other, you don't want to go overboard into Harlequin Romance territory. After all, you're shooting for genuine tears, not tears of laughter. Toeing the line is no easy business. The following tips will get you on the way to writing your vows with confidence, a critical component to the perfect declaration of intent.

1. Think back on all the endearments and pledges you've already made to your fiancé. There's good material there just waiting to be recycled.
2. Read over any love letters, faxes, or e-mails your fiancé might have sent you. If you don't think those are over the top, then why should anything you say be any different?
3. Don't fret over every last word as you write. First get your point across, then edit the vow, and replace any phrases or words you might find objectionable.
4. Silence your inner censor with a glass of wine (or two), and proceed to boldly go where you've never dared go before.
5. Remember Darva Conger's vow to Rick Rockwell (of *Who Wants to Marry a Multi-Millionaire?* notoriety) and realize that no matter what you say, it won't be nearly as tacky.

rite of spring? Or is it the month of your anniversary as a couple? Maybe you two met in April and would like to impart the significance of this special time to your guests. And imagine the possibilities if both of your still-happily-married parents' weddings took place in April—talk about carrying on an auspicious tradition.

If, however, there's nothing particularly symbolic about the month of your wedding, it might just be that you two like the weather at this time of year. That too is worth mentioning, especially if the month of your wedding is December—only two soulmates such as yourselves could find anything to favor about this decidedly frosty time of the year. Of course, this might very well be an off-season wedding, and your top three concerns for having chosen December were budget, budget, and budget. Don't worry, a few words about starting with as little foliage as a botanic garden in winter and blossoming together as a married couple could get your vows up and running. For some ideas about how to incorporate the time of year into your vows, look no further than Chapter 11, where all twelve months are represented.

Two Vows with One Pen

Whereas composing two sets of personalized vows can be the best way to reflect the individual dreams and beliefs of each partner, shared vows are symbolic in their own way. Agreeing to make the same declaration is something akin to a joint mission statement, your way of telling the world that you're of one mind on the subject of marriage. To be sure, this does not mean that one of you will do all the work and the other will take half the credit, but you might find that coming up with a single statement is considerably less time consuming. After all, two heads are better than one.

A Most Pleasant Surprise

If you want to work with your partner to come up with your wedding vows, there's nothing to stop you. But if you want your declaration to seem unscripted and carry the stamp of spontaneity, you may decide to surprise your loved one on your wedding day. You need not go out of your way to carry out this sneak attack; simply insist upon writing your vows alone and then don't disclose them until the grand unveiling. Of course, the surprise should go both ways, so you'll have to convince your fiancé to follow suit. If you talk up the romantic aspects of this kind of vow exchange, you shouldn't have any problem in the persuasion department.

Lighten Up!

Although this is no time to make attempts at humor, the natural course of the vow-composing process may lead you to certain statements that will bring a smile to your guests' lips. Worse things have been known to happen. Perhaps the way you two met was funny, or maybe there's something amusing about your courtship or the location of your ceremony. No matter how amusing the anecdote, if it's important to you and your fiancé, feel free to include it in your vows. Exchanging vows is a serious business, to be sure, but weddings are a celebration of life, so don't feel as if you have to mirror the often somber quality of traditional vows when creating your own.

Not Without Your Intended

With the bride up to her elbows in wedding planning, it sometimes seems as if the groom is getting off scot-free. Well, here's your chance to turn the tables. While some grooms have been known to press their luck, you should put your foot down: There's no way you're writing the vows for both of you, even if he does insist that you're a much better writer.

To bring him on board, start off with a grand buildup. This vow-writing thing is going to be fun. You'll order in pizza, pick up a six-pack of his favorite beer, and once the brainstorming is over, you'll reward yourselves with a movie or a night out on the town. If he's still trying to procrastinate or shirk his duty, you might have to get tough. Creating your wedding vows is best not left to the very last minute.

Set the scene for a romantic afternoon or evening. A clean, tidy space, some low-key mood music, and a supply of provisions are imperative. Incense and a candle or two wouldn't hurt either. While you're at it, consider ordering a nice meal to go with those candles—creativity does not live on love alone.

A picnic is also a nice way to get your creative juices flowing. You can either surprise your partner or organize the outing together. Just remember, once you've laid out your spread and enjoyed the contents of your wicker basket, it's time to set to the task of composing your vows. In other words, leave that Frisbee at home.

Some Guidelines

You've probably discussed the more serious aspects of marriage and your relationship already, but refreshing your memory is critical at this stage of the game. If they are to mean anything at all, your personalized vows must be grounded in the fundamentals of your relationship. If you're having trouble getting started, this section should get you up and running in no time.

When creating your own vows, start by writing down answers to the following questions. Doing so will provide you with valuable source material—and help you develop the vow you're looking for:

(Answer together) How do you, as a couple, define the following terms?

Love _____

_____

Trust_____

_____

Marriage _____

_____

Family _____

_____

Commitment _____

_____

Togetherness _____

_____

(Answer together) How did the two of you first meet?

_____

_____

_____

_____

_____

_____

(Answer separately) What was the first thing you noticed about your partner?

Bride:

_____
_____
_____
_____
_____
_____

Groom:

_____
_____
_____
_____
_____
_____

(Answer together) List here any shared hobbies or other mutual interests you have.

_____
_____
_____
_____
_____
_____
_____
_____
_____

(Answer together) What was the single most important event in your relationship? (Or, what was the event that you feel says the most about your development as a couple?)

_____

_____

_____

_____

_____

_____

(Answer together) How similar (or different) were your respective childhoods? Take a moment and try to recount some of the important parallels or differences here.

_____

_____

_____

_____

_____

(Answer together) Is there a song, poem, or book that is particularly meaningful in your relation-ship? If so, identify it here.

_____

_____

_____

_____

_____

_____

(Answer together) Do you and your partner share a common religious tradition? If so, identify it here.

_____

_____

_____

_____

_____

_____

(Answer together) If you share a common religious tradition, is there a particular scriptural passage that you as a couple find particularly meaningful? If so, identify it here.

_____

_____

_____

_____

_____

_____

(Answer together) Why did your parents' marriages succeed or fail? What marital pitfalls do you want to avoid? What can you take from your parents' examples, good or bad?

_____

_____

_____

_____

_____

_____

(Answer together) Take some time to reminisce about the course of your relationship. When did you first realize you loved each other? When did you first say the words? What trials and tribulations has your love had to overcome? What shared memories are you most fond of?

_____

_____

_____

_____

_____

(Answer separately) What do you love about your partner? Why?

Bride:

_____

_____

_____

_____

_____

Groom:

_____

_____

_____

_____

_____

(Answer together) How do you and your partner
look at personal growth and change? What aspects
of your life together are likely to change over the
coming years? How do you anticipate dealing with
those changes? How important is mutual respect
and tolerance in your relationship? When one of
you feels that a particular need is being over-
looked, what do you feel is the best way to
address this problem with the other person?

_____

_____

_____

_____

_____

_____

_____

_____

(Answer together) Do you and your partner have
a common vision of what your life as older
people will be like? Will it include children or
grandchildren? Take this opportunity to put into
words the vision you and your partner share of
what it will be like to grow old together.

_____

_____

_____

_____

_____

_____

_____

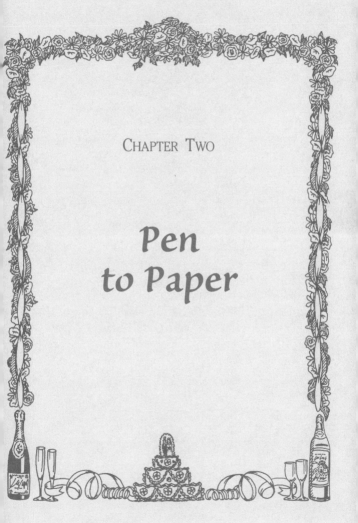

CHAPTER TWO

Pen
to Paper

*N*ow that you and your fiancé have spent several hours in deep conversation, you're ready to tackle the blank sheets of paper that will soon house your most intimate thoughts on love and devotion everlasting. Your lengthy discussion has no doubt led to a greater and more profound understanding of your relationship. You're certainly more aware of the values and dreams that you share as a couple. It's this kind of insight that's going to make your vow stand out as a sincere pledge of allegiance and not just a hodgepodge of meaningless phrases and hollow words.

So without further ado, it's time to roll up your sleeves, pick up a pen, and get down to the business of composing your masterpiece.

Draft One: There Are No Rules

Using the material you have developed, set about the task of writing a first draft of your unique wedding vow.

Let yourself go—there is no right or wrong way to write your wedding vow. Give yourself permission to write anything and everything that seems right—you can always cut text back later on. Go ahead and wax rhapsodic. Feel free to write anything, the more outlandish the better. Thrust yourself into the free associating frame of mind. Let your stream of consciousness run wild, and get carried away by its powerful current. Since this is a very rough draft, take advantage of the opportunity to rant like a madman. Hold nothing back. Don't be surprised if it takes you a few drafts to develop a vow that is right for you.

After you've finished writing your first draft, read it over. But be forewarned: No matter how sappy your ramblings may sound, resist the urge to crumple, tear, or burn the draft. While certain passages may bring on a feeling of nausea or elicit spontaneous bursts of uncontrollable laughter, at least a few phrases should smack of sheer genius and stand out as vow-worthy. Highlight these gems for possible future use.

Method to the Madness

The first draft was all about jogging your imagination and sharpening your creative instincts. But, let's face it, you're probably not going to want to recite it before total strangers, much less a hundred of your nearest and dearest. What you need now is a little structure, and there's nothing like an outline to get your thoughts organized.

Approach this as if you're writing a research paper, albeit a very short one, on a subject you're intimately familiar with and 100 percent passionate about. Envision your vows in their entirety—from the opening lines to the closing sentiments—and begin to systematically write each part until you've said your piece.

The Seven Outlines of Highly Effective Vow-Writers

Far be it from us to tell you how to run your wedding. Look at these outlines and examples simply as blueprints geared to get your vows up and running. Of course, you may decide to do something completely different, something no one has ever seen before, something that no one in attendance is likely to ever forget. More power to you, no one ever said that structure is for everyone.

You need not follow any particular form or pattern, but if you feel more comfortable doing so, you may want to consider working within one of the following outlines.

Outline One

Groom: (Initial statement relating to past.)
Bride: (Initial statement relating to past.)
Groom: (Statement relating to partner.)
Bride: (Statement relating to partner.)
Groom: (Promise or commitment in terms you feel are appropriate for your relationship.)
Bride: (Promise or commitment in terms you feel are appropriate for your relationship.)

Example

Groom: When I was a child, I thought nothing would ever persuade me to leave my home state of Maine when it came time to make my way in the world. But that was before I met you.
Bride: As a young girl, I dreamed of a place where I could grow with another, step by step, side by side. I have found that place in your heart.
Groom: Kathy, you have helped me to learn that love is a direction, and not a destination.
Bride: John, you have taught me that, when someone is there no matter what, trust and commitment come without effort, of their own accord.
Groom: I pledge to you my future. I will share all my tomorrows with you and no other.
Bride: I pledge to you my future. I will share all my tomorrows with you and no other.

Outline Two

Groom: (Extended statement incorporating important materials developed in answering the questions above, and culminating in a statement of your commitment to one another.)

Bride: (Extended statement incorporating important materials developed in answering the questions above, and culminating in a statement of your commitment to one another.)

Example

Groom: The first thing I noticed about Kathy was her radiant smile. We were both auditioning for a show in college, and when I asked her what type of piece she'd prepared, she said she planned to make it all up on the spot—and then she smiled at me. Kathy, your warmth and spontaneity have won my heart utterly. From this day forward, I will stand by your side. You are the one I will be true to always. Let us make our lives together.

Bride: The first thing I noticed about John was his unceasing energy. As he waited for the director to call him in, he couldn't seem to sit still, and when I told him my plans for the audition, he stared at me as though I were mad—but mad in an interesting way. What he didn't tell you just now was that I got the lead role in that show and he wound up in the chorus. But John, from that day to this, and for all the days that follow, you will always be my leading man. From this day forward, I will stand by your side. You are the one I will be true to always. Let us make our lives together.

Outline Three

Bride: (Opening verse of a favorite song, or quote from a book or poem that is particularly meaningful to you as a couple.)

Groom: (Continuation of cited material.)

Bride: (Continuation of cited material.)

Groom: (Continuation of cited material.)

Bride: (Promise or commitment in terms you feel are appropriate for your relationship.)

Groom: (Promise or commitment in terms you feel are appropriate for your relationship.)

Example

Bride: Grow old along with me!

Groom: The best is yet to be.

Bride: The last of life, for which the first was made.

Groom: Our times are in his hand Who saith, A whole I planned; Youth shows but half. Trust God; see all, nor be afraid!

Bride: God bless our love.

Groom: God bless our love.

Bride: John, in this assembly of friends and family, I take you today as my husband. I do this in the certainty of my soul,

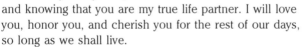

and knowing that you are my true life partner. I will love you, honor you, and cherish you for the rest of our days, so long as we shall live.

Groom: Kathy, in this assembly of friends and family, I take you today as my wife. I do this in the certainty of my soul, and knowing that you are my true life partner. I will love you, honor you, and cherish you for the rest of our days, so long as we shall live.

Outline Four

Bride: (Dictionary definition of an important aspect of your relationship.)

Groom: (Elaboration on this theme, extending into your own interpretation, as a couple, of the word or phrase.)

Bride: (Promise or commitment in terms you feel are appropriate for your relationship.)

Groom: (Promise or commitment in terms you feel are appropriate for your relationship.)

Example

Bride: The dictionary defines love as the attraction or affection felt for a person who elicits delight and admiration.

Groom: For us, as we begin our lives together, that definition is only a beginning. We make a commitment to our love today, and we see it as a willingness to give, to see oneself through another, and to work together to make the best of parts of ourselves a reality.

Bride: John, my love for you is the foundation upon which I want to build my life. Take this ring as a sign of my faith.

Groom: Kathy, my love for you is the foundation upon which I want to build my life. Take this ring as a sign of my faith.

Outline Five

Groom: (Brief statement acknowledging and celebrating the gathering of friends and family.)

Bride: (Longer statement continuing this idea.)

Groom: (Promise or commitment in terms you feel are appropriate for your relationship.)

Bride: (Promise or commitment in terms you feel are appropriate for your relationship.)

Example

Groom: Today we bring two families together—and celebrate as one family.

Bride: To all who have come with us to mark our union today, we offer our thanks for your help through the years, our embrace for your support over the weeks and months that led to this day, and our promise that, as new members of this new and larger family, we will always be there for you as you have been there for us.

Groom: Kathy, in joining my life with yours, I give you all that I am and all that I may become. I give myself to you as your husband.

Bride: John, in joining my life with yours, I give you all that I am and all that I may become. I give myself to you as your wife.

Outline Six

Bride: (Scriptural passage that is particularly meaningful to you as a couple.)

Groom: (Continuation of cited material.)

Bride: (Continuation of cited material.)

Groom: (Continuation of cited material.)

Bride: (Continuation of cited material.)

Groom: (Continuation of cited material.)

Bride: (Promise or commitment in terms you feel are appropriate for your relationship.)

Groom: (Promise or commitment in terms you feel are appropriate for your relationship.)

Example

Groom: From the beginning of creation God made them male and female.

Bride: This is why a man must leave father and mother . . .

Groom: . . . and the two become one body. They are no longer two, therefore, but one body.

Bride: So then, what God has united . . .

Groom: . . . man must not divide.

Bride: John, today, in the gathering of this honored company, we unite in God's love. I pledge myself to you as your wife, and will be faithful to you for all of our days.

Groom: Kathy, today, in the gathering of this honored company, we unite in God's love. I pledge myself to you as your husband, and will be faithful to you for all of our days.

Outline Seven

(With your partner, develop a single paragraph, of whatever length you feel is appropriate, to be recited by both partners. The paragraph should draw on the material you have written in answer to the questions on earlier pages.)

Example

I, (name), take you, (name), to be my (husband/wife). I want to grow old along with you; I want to share the blessings of children and family with you. Today, before these honored guests and beloved family members, I vow to love you and honor you for as long as we both live. I vow to respect you, listen to you, and grow with you, through good times and bad times.

Be Creative!

Remember: The right way to compose your own wedding vows is your way. The outlines and examples you have just seen are offered as general guidelines only. In customizing your own wedding vows, you are always best advised to let your own imagination be your guide. Develop vows that are meaningful to both you and your partner, that say something unique about your love, and that take the form that best exemplifies the way you envision your new life together.

Word to the Wise

Stay away from negative imagery. Your vows have to be inspirational and uplifting, not ominous and foreboding. So, when you start writing, try to think about all the positive qualities that you have to bring to your marriage, instead of focusing on all those dastardly deeds that you wouldn't be caught dead doing. The following example should serve as a marital vow don't:

> I, Kathy, take you, John, to be my husband from this day forward. I promise never to stray from the path that we forge as we face our tomorrows together as one. This wedding is a true joining of souls. Although we've had our ups and downs in the past, our lawful union will not outlast the love, trust, and harmony that exist between us today. I promise to be vigilant in preserving these, our shared values, as the mainstays of our marriage no matter what manner of hardship comes our way.

If you're wondering what's wrong with this vow, we implore you to look again. This time, however, we've taken the trouble of italicizing the offending segments.

I, Kathy, take you, John, to be my husband from this day forward. I promise *never to stray from* the path that we forge as we face our tomorrows together as one. This wedding is a true joining of souls. Although we've had our *ups and downs in the past*, our lawful *union will not outlast the love, trust, and harmony* that exist between us today. I promise to be vigilant in preserving these, our shared values, as the mainstays of our marriage *no matter what manner of hardship comes our way*.

First of all, the words *never* and *not* have no place in a wedding vow. All the things you're not going to do, to maintain the sanctity of your marriage, go without saying on your wedding day. Instead of "never to stray from," for instance, Kathy could have easily written "stay faithful to."

Equally irrelevant are the arguments and breakups that you and your spouse-to-be may have had in the past. Unless you're referring to the time you helped your fiancé through an illness in the family, or something of this nature, mentioning past "ups and downs" is completely uncalled for.

Finally, alluding to future turmoil—as Kathy does when she says that the "union will not outlast the love, trust, and harmony" and "no matter what hardship comes our way"— is also a great way to rain on your own parade. Even the somber, traditional vows attempt to neutralize life's less sunshiny aspects by pairing "for poorer" with "for richer" and "in sickness" with "in health." So, if you want this to go down as one of the happiest days of your life, by all means, remain optimistic. In other chapters of this book, you will find many quotes, poems, and scriptural passages.

Quick Fix for Momentary Writer's Block

Every day, we're called upon to think of unique solutions to common problems. With a little creativity, we manage to overcome and move on to the next hurdle. Writing your wedding vows, however, is an altogether different proposition. You'll need to tap into all of your creative energy to find the perfect words. Although you'll find more intensive creativity-enhancing exercises in the next chapter, the following pointers can't be beat if you're only slightly on the stumped side.

1. Remove yourself from the blatantly empty page—take a bath, run a mile, just get away from the offensively unmarred sheet of paper.
2. Look over old photographs of you and your beloved.
3. If you're used to working on a computer, go the old-fashioned route with a pen (and vice versa).
4. Close your eyes and draw a picture of you and your fiancé at the altar; pay special attention to the images that spring to mind.
5. Two words: Snack break.

The Right Words

As you begin to write your vows, it's not unusual to find yourself at a loss for words. The following vocabulary list should help jump-start your thought process and pick up where "The Seven Outlines of Highly Effective Vow-Writers" left off.

A
Absolute
Admire
Adore
Affection
Allegiance
Alliance
Always
Anticipate
Ardor
Attraction

B
Beauty
Benevolence
Bliss
Bold
Bond
Bounty

C
Camaraderie
Caring
Ceaseless

Charm
Cherish
Companionship
Compassion
Connection
Constant
Content
Cosmic
Cultivate

D
Dedication
Delight
Desire
Destiny
Devotion
Dignity
Divine
Dream

E
Elation
Elegance
Emotion

Empathy
Endless
Enduring
Energy
Engaging
Esteem
Eternal
Eternity
Ethical
Everlasting
Exquisite

F
Faith
Fanciful
Fidelity
Fondly
Forever
Forthright
Foster
Frank
Friendship
Fun

Date: 10/1/2018 9:43am
Member: Wayne S. Cone

Title	Author	Due
The everything wedding v	Anastasio, Ja	10/22
Vows & toasts: hundreds		10/22
The wedding ceremony pla	Johnson, Judi	10/22

Total items currently out: 3.

Wow! Today, you saved $39.85.
n 2018, you have saved $91.

?7-18 @10am After School: Erupting Art

G
Gaiety
Generous
Gentle
Genuine
Gift
Glad
Glorious
Godly
Grace
Grandeur
Grant
Gratitude
Gravity

H
Happiness
Harmony
Heart
Heartfelt
Heavenly
Highlight
Holy
Honest
Honor
Hope
Humor

I
Ideal
Immortal

Impervious
Independent
Indestructible
Infinite
Insightful
Inspire
Integrity
Intense
Invaluable

J
Join
Jovial
Joy
Jubilation
Judgment

K
Karma
Keenly
Key
Kiss
Knowledge

L
Lasting
Laughter
Life
Lifetime
Light
Limitless

Love
Loyal

M
Magical
Marry
Marvel
Mate
Mature
Meaningful
Meld
Merge
Moral

N
Natural
Never-ending
Noble
Nuptial

O
Oceanic
Oneness
Open
Optimism
Overcome

P
Partner
Passion
Peaceful

Perfection
Permanence
Playful
Pleasure
Pledge
Poise
Precious
Predetermined
Preserve
Priceless
Promise
Protect
Provide
Pure
Purpose

Q
Quality

R
Radiant
Rare
Real
Refresh
Regard
Rejoice
Rekindle
Renew
Resolve
Respect

Responsibility
Righteous

S
Sacred
Sacrifice
Sanctity
Selfless
Serene
Sincerity
Soul
Soulmate
Special
Spirit
Splendid
Spousal
Steadfast
Stimulate
Sublime
Suited
Sympathy

T
Tender
Thankful
Total
Treasure
True
Trust

U
Ultimate
Unearthly
Unify
Union
United
Universal
Uplifting
Utopia

V
Value
Vibrant
Virtuous
Vision
Vivacious
Vow

W
Warm
Wedlock
Whole
Wisdom
Wish
Wondrous
Worthy

Z
Zeal
Zenith
Zest

First Draft of Our Wedding Vows

_____
_____
_____
_____
_____
_____
_____
_____
_____
_____
_____
_____
_____
_____
_____
_____
_____
_____
_____
_____
_____
_____
_____
_____
_____
_____
_____
_____
_____
_____
_____
_____
_____
_____
_____
_____

Second Draft of Our Wedding Vows

_____
_____
_____
_____
_____
_____
_____
_____
_____
_____
_____
_____
_____
_____
_____
_____
_____
_____
_____
_____
_____
_____
_____
_____
_____
_____
_____
_____
_____
_____
_____
_____
_____
_____
_____
_____
_____
_____

Third Draft of Our Wedding Vows

_____
_____
_____
_____
_____
_____
_____
_____
_____
_____
_____
_____
_____
_____
_____
_____
_____
_____
_____
_____
_____
_____
_____
_____
_____
_____
_____
_____
_____
_____
_____
_____
_____
_____
_____

CHAPTER THREE

Break
Out
of the Box

"What box?" you wonder. Well, let's just say that if you have to ask, you're probably ready to skip on to the next chapters. The following pages contain emergency creativity repair treatments. While we all use our creative thought processes to put out fires on the job, plan outings with friends and the like, only poets and writers channel their creativity into the written word on a daily basis. In all probability, you haven't written a poem since high school English, and your e-mails are hammered out in only the most workmanlike of fashions. There's no shame in admitting it, so you might as well fess up—your imagination is in a state of hibernation. The sooner you come to grips with this harsh reality, the quicker you'll snap out of it.

Although we're all blessed with a boundless well of imagination, the passage of time can make us forget the once familiar route to this watering hole of creativity. Some of us have to work at recovering our long lost wellspring of creative thought, organizing search parties and orchestrating elaborate quests in pursuit of this El Dorado. And that, in a nutshell, is what this chapter is all about.

Stop and Smell the Roses

As you prepare to reclaim the creativity that is your birthright, your first order of business is to make an active effort to remain cool, calm, and collected. High pressure and free-flowing spontaneous bursts of creative energy don't make for any type of bedfellows, strange or otherwise. Thus, the best time to reconnect with your imagination is on a weekend or a day off from work, a time when there's nothing to be done but to take naps after breakfast, watch *E! True Hollywood Story* marathons, and catch up on the classics of Western literature.

Needless to say, you won't be doing any of that on this particular day off. Instead, you'll be waking up to your first morning of pure enjoyment. The first hour of your day should be spent looking out your window and learning to appreciate the view (this might prove difficult for some of our good-view-deprived readers, but nothing is impossible). Pull up a window seat and savor your breakfast coffee without the aid of Katie Couric, today's *Times,* or this week's issue of *U.S. News and World Report.* Take in the architecture, follow the goings on of pedestrians as they mill about your intersection, watch your neighbor's kid mow the lawn. Listen to the sounds of the area, the bees buzzing, the birds chirping, the cars honking, the sirens blaring. Whether your aural landscape is a pastoral dream or a big city headache, your task is to pay attention and find the beauty in it.

Feeling Like a Kid Again

After about an hour of this passive observation, you may very well find yourself climbing the walls with sheer boredom. The restless energy will be coursing through your veins, and "ants in your pants" will be the only way to describe your desperate-for-something-to-do state of mind. Congratulations and welcome to the mentality of a three-year-old. They can't read, they take only a passing interest in television, and as far as work is concerned, they don't yet know the full meaning of the word (bless their giddy little hearts). And we wonder why they have such vivid imaginations!

While your first post-view-enjoyment impulse may be to lunge for the nearest magazine, you must resist it at all costs. You cannot read, watch TV, play a musical instrument, or listen to your CD collection. Neither can you call your fiancé and your friends to complain about this ridiculous exercise. Not yet anyway.

Bored as you are, you must resign yourself to the only entertainment available to a person of your scant resources—playing make-believe. Are you ready?

Rack Your Brain

If you think we're going to tell you how to spend the next two hours of your life, think again. This is your time to do whatever you want, short of the things you do to pass time on a regular basis. If you want to escape into a dream world, wherein you'd waltz through your wedding day with all the grace of Fred and Ginger, try on every outfit in your closet and prance before the full-length mirror, choreograph a dance routine and commit it to motor memory, or ponder all the options you'd have if you won $100 million in the lottery, have at it. However, we must urge you not to make any attempts at writing at this time, whether it be love songs, plays, or the Great American Novel.

If you're still hard-pressed for activity, all is not lost. We've come up with a few arts-and-crafts exercises, any of which should keep you occupied while shifting your pursuit of imagination into high gear.

The "We Were, Are, and Will Be" Collage: Get out your poster board and draw an outline of you and your fiancé. It doesn't have to be a masterpiece, the best you can do should suffice. Now grab a scissors and some magazines. Proceed to flip through the glossy pages (pay no mind to the articles, the pictures are the thing!) and, working from left to right, begin pasting the images that best represent how you view your relationship at its start, at the present time, and in the future. Don't limit yourself to pictures, if you see certain colors and words that define the stages of your romance, feel free to incorporate.

Picket Fences: On a plain white sheet of paper, draw a picture of your dream house. Use colored crayons or pencils and make the walls transparent so you can see inside. Don't try to be realistic; fill the house with whatever you want.

Mix Your Metaphors: Your wedding is a major life-altering event. Can you think of something in nature, be it animal, vegetable, or mineral, that goes through a similar transformation? Go ahead and draw a picture of it, and don't be a scrimp with the colors.

The Great Outdoors

Now that you've been cooped up for three hours with nothing but arts and crafts and your imagination to amuse you, you're probably dying to get outside and make some snow angels, or sand castles for that matter. Whatever the season, you're never going to find a better time to enjoy all that nature has to offer. You've got two full hours in which to indulge your yen for fresh air, so get to it because time's a'wastin'.

As you wander the streets and promenades, keep your eyes peeled. You've probably traversed the same route on countless occasions, but have you really taken the time to notice all the small things that make your neck of the city or housing development unique? In all likelihood, you're far too busy to concern yourself with such trifles on a daily basis. The following guidelines should start you thinking in the right direction:

Why Ask Why: Pretend that you've just learned the meaning of the word "why" and ask away. Why does the sign say "Don't Walk" when there are no cars in sight? Why do the geese come to the man-made pond on the corner every time this year? Why is that strange man talking to a brown paper bag?

Make up your own answers, with no regard to the laws of urban planning, environmental science, or common sense. Try to give answers that tell a story, and see if your time outside doesn't turn into something quite extraordinary.

Give It a Name: Think of this as "I Spy," the freestyle version. Look around at everything you're used to calling a "thingamajig" and try to give it a proper name. If one doesn't spring to mind, try to name it yourself. For instance, if you happen to notice the rubber edges on revolving doors, you can decide to call them "abberdecks." Name at least three items before heading for home.

People and Places: While you're out and about, take some time to observe the passers-by. Take note of everything from what they're wearing to how they carry themselves. What secrets lurk behind their seemingly placid facial expressions? Where are they going? Where have they been? Every person is a mystery just waiting to be solved, and so is every park bench, street corner, and suburban home. Try to imagine what goes on behind the closed front doors. Consider all the little dramas that might have unfolded at the Washington and Elm intersection. Reflect upon all the romances that might have come alive beneath that hundred-year-old oak tree.

Back at the Drawing Board

Once you're back inside, bask in the comfort of your own four walls. But don't touch that dial or check that voice mail. Inspiration waits for no man or woman, so take out a pencil and get to writing your vows. All of you who fretted about coming up with the right words before need worry no more. Your powers of imagination are now at their peak, and squandering these precious moments on anything resembling *Entertainment Tonight* or your friends' rambling phone messages might just land you right back at ground zero.

To prepare yourself for the formidable task that lies ahead, you should follow these guidelines to the letter.

1. Off the hook. You guessed it: Disconnect your phone, turn off your cellular, and, in the name of all that's holy, put away that pager. The last thing you need when you're in the middle of writing the greatest single sentence you've ever written, is to hear your friends calling to complain about their bosses.

2. Soundproof booth. Discerning the voice of your muse will be no easy matter if she's got to compete with the noise from the street and the pitter-patter of your roommate's four-inch heels. Close your door, shut your windows, and drown out the more stubborn sound waves with the sound of music (classical, jazz, New Age . . . as long as it doesn't have lyrics, anything will do).

3. Settle in for the long haul. If you sneak off in search of the refrigerator every time words seem to be failing you, you're not going to finish the

deed before you, much less manage to squeeze into your tux or gown come wedding day. Stay put until you're satisfied with what you've wrought. One short break is all you're entitled to, so use it wisely.

4. It's about goals. Recall the "Seven Outlines of Highly Effective Vow-Writers" that were listed in Chapter 2. Whether you go back to consult these or devise an original outline of your own, make sure to set up a series of steps that will let you know that you're making progress toward completing what can sometimes seem like an overwhelming task.

5. Think positive. If you approach the work with uncertainty and doubt, the vows will suffer. Likewise if you assume an annoyed and petulant attitude. While this is important, it's not astrophysics—you can do it and it is fun.

Last Words of Advice

As you begin to apply yourself to your vows, do not feel compelled to keep your pencil in perpetual motion. Since it's about the quality and not the quantity of your writing, thought, silent and still, will probably take up most of your time. No doubt, you'll also find yourself doing a great deal of research, flipping through the following pages and consulting other texts that you find personally relevant. This is to be expected and shouldn't cause you any discomfort until such time as three hours have passed and you've still to write so much as a phrase (at which point, we recommend you stop procrastinating, hop on your pencil, and write like the wind).

The following aids should inspire you to put in your best work yet.

1. Today's arts-and-crafts projects: You didn't really believe that we'd have you put forth all that effort if there wasn't going to be some wedding-vow-related payoff, now did you?

    If you made a "We Were, Are, Will Be" collage, you're a natural storyteller. Pay special attention to the images and words you chose to feature in your project. If you look long enough, you'll find that these tell a special kind of love story, and it just might be one that deserves to be summarized in your vows.

    Those of you who chose to draw a "Picket Fences" picture should understand that your decision reflects your hopeful and wishful state of mind. Your dreams are important to you, so don't be shy about incorporating these into your wedding vows.

    Whoever went the way of "Mix Your Metaphors" is a poet at heart. But half of your poem has already been completed. Look at your picture of this morning and consider what it is that you compared your wedding day to. Go with this insight, not only including it in your vows, but elaborating and building upon it to create a true love poem.

    As you look at your morning's artwork, note the colors that you used and try to connect these to the feelings and emotions you might be experiencing as you approach your wedding day. Again, these might merit inclusion in your vows.

2. Something borrowed: Will Shakespeare had good reason to warn against borrowing; history has yet to witness a more imposed-upon scribe. But one man's loss is another's gain, so feel free to rifle through this book's lengthy collection of quotes for inspiration. Just one brilliant sentence can open the floodgates to your creative process. Now, is borrowing one little phrase tantamount to plagiarism? Not according to most experts who tend to agree with the maxim that all's fair in love.

   While you can, of course, use all of Edmund Spenser's poem, you could also choose to crib a solitary line, such as "Let baser things devise to lie in dust, but you shall live by fame." From that point on, you can carry on however you like, writing your own heartfelt, if not anthology-worthy, poem in the process. For instance, "Let baser things devise to lie in dust, but you shall live by fame, for I vow to celebrate your virtues and glorify your name. But, whether toiling in obscurity or renowned throughout, you'll always be the only one whom I can't live without."

Use the space on the following page to draft your personalized wedding vows. Have fun and may the spirit of the occasion move you!

CHAPTER FOUR

A Ceremony
All Your Own

riting your own wedding vows is a great beginning, but why stop there? Believe it or not, you can suit the whole ceremony to your specifications if you so wish, provided of course that your officiant doesn't have any objections. Retooling the entire ceremony will mean more writing work for you and your partner, but if it means making the proceedings more meaningful, then no effort is too great.

You'd be surprised at just how many couples are choosing to craft their own wedding ceremonies from start to finish. Whether it's due to a desire to break new ground, an aversion to strict formality, a lack of religious belief, or a yearning for a more spiritually satisfying ceremony, more and more people are turning tradition on its ear and delighting their wedding guests with something quite unexpected.

In fact, the ceremony has only two parts that are not up for debate: the declarations of intent, in which each partner agrees to the marriage, and the pronouncement of marriage, in which you're pronounced husband and wife. Everything else, from the opening address to the words spoken during the ring exchange, can be tweaked and adapted to your unique situation. Even ceremonies that stick to traditional guidelines need not be strictly by-the-numbers affairs. By including supplementary readings and music, or omitting certain parts of the proceeding altogether, couples can concoct a service that is in keeping with their beliefs, personalities, and lifestyles.

Traditional Weddings from A to Z

To successfully update your wedding ceremony, you need a firm grasp on the various ingredients that go into the making of a standard ceremony. Up to now, much of the talk has focused on wedding vows, but while these are important, they are by no means the alpha and omega of the wedding service. The ceremony, in all its entirety, breaks down as follows:

- ✍ Introduction/greeting: The officiant greets the guests and calls attention to the solemn nature of marriage and the wedding vows and asks all assembled to respect the union in a charge to the convocation.

- ✍ Opening prayers: A higher power is invoked by the officiant to witness the ceremony and bless the union.

- ✍ Address: The officiant's statements to the couple and the guests on the meaning of marriage.

- ✍ The declaration of consent/intent: These are the so-called "I dos" whereby both partners assert that they enter into the marriage by their own volition.

- ✍ Presentation of the bride: Officiant asks the person giving the bride away to stand up.

- ✍ Vows: The cornerstone of the ceremony, in which the bride and groom address each other and promise to fulfill their roles as husband and wife.

🎗 Ring exchange: The traditional act of exchanging wedding rings, meant to symbolize an eternal union.

🎗 Pronouncement of marriage: Wherein the officiant pronounces the bride and groom husband and wife. Usually followed by a kiss.

Mix 'n' Match

Keep in mind that the wedding ceremony is a formula that's made to be tampered with. If we seem to be harping on this point, it's only because it cannot be stressed enough. You can write your own vows, delete whole sections, move certain parts around, and decide to include music and readings wherever you feel is appropriate. Many couples stop at writing their own wedding vows, while others also write their ring-exchange vows and even guide the words of the officiant. The point is that it's entirely up to you. You can stray as far from the charted course as humanly possible or take the unconventional but conservative approach demonstrated by the recently married Wade and Mitie.

Model Ceremony: Marriage Ceremony for Mitie and Wade

℘ (Introduction/Greeting)

Welcome. We are here to witness and celebrate the love and marriage of Mitie and Wade. We their family and friends form a community of love so that we may support them in their lives together.

℘ (Declaration of Consent)

Wade, will you have this woman to be your wife, to live together in the covenant of marriage? Will you love her, comfort her, honor and keep her in sickness and in health, and forsaking all others, to be faithful to her as long as you both shall live?

Mitie, will you have this man to be your husband, to live together in the covenant of marriage? Will you love him, comfort him, honor and keep him in sickness and in health, and forsaking all others, to be faithful to him as long as you both shall live?

℘ (Charge to the convocation)

Will all of you witnessing these promises do all in your power to uphold these two persons in their marriage?

℘ (Address)

There is a much greater motivation in solemnizing a relationship in marriage than spoken words. For marriage will bind the two of you together for life in a relationship so close and so intimate that it will profoundly influence your whole future. Marriage is a commitment given freely and without reservation. The union of husband and wife in heart, body, and mind is intended for their mutual joy; for the help and comfort given one another in prosperity and adversity. The essence of this commitment is the taking of another person in his or her entirety as lover, companion, and friend. It is, therefore, a decision that is not to be entered into lightly but rather undertaken with great consideration and respect for both the other person and oneself. If you remember to give each other kindness and understanding, then an abiding faith and love will be yours.

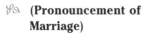 **(Readings—recited by different friends)**

> Neruda, Sonnet 17
> Shakespeare, Sonnet 116
> e. e. cummings, 225

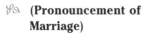 **(Vows)**

> I, Wade/Mitie, promise to love, cherish, support, and protect you, to stand by you always and to create a loving family with you. All that I have and all that I am I give to you.

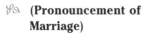 **(Music)**

> Nancy sings "Amazing Grace."

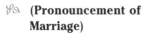 **(Ring Exchange)**

> Wade (repeats after judge): "This ring I give you in token and pledge of my constant faith and abiding love."
>
> Mitie (repeats after judge): "This ring I give you in token and pledge of my constant faith and abiding love."

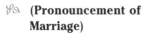 **(Pronouncement of Marriage)**

The Sound of Music

Asking your friends to sing and read should add some good old-fashioned fun to the ceremony, but believe it or not, there's still more you can do to ensure that your guests don't drift off into reveries of the reception while the ceremony is still in full swing. Even the most solemn wedding can benefit from a carefully selected soundtrack. After all, well-chosen music, just like well-chosen words, can provide atmosphere and enhance the mood and meaning of your ceremony from start to finish.

Most marrying couples don't give much thought to ceremony music. With the exception of "Here Comes the Bride" (and a few other stray notes from the organ), there aren't too many pieces of music directly associated with the ceremony. But these days, more and more couples are spicing up their ceremony with a variety of songs, musicians, and singers. If these are options you'd like to consider, consult with the officiant in charge of your ceremony as soon as possible. Some religions place restrictions on secular selections during the ceremony, but others may be very open to them. Ask about this well in advance.

Your best bet for finding appropriate ceremony music is to check with the musical coordinator for the ceremony site. Most religious facilities have a staff organist or choir director who can help you choose the best possible music given his or her experience. The coordinator can also recommend singers and musicians who have performed well at other ceremonies. Don't worry if you think you don't know enough about classical or "church" music; the musicians you eventually choose can offer suggestions based on the guidelines you set forth.

Before you hire a full orchestra to accompany the church choir, though, remember that the cost of musicians and singers for the ceremony must fit into your overall music budget. It may take some planning, but don't be intimidated—you can have wonderful music for both the ceremony and the reception with a little compromise and ingenuity.

Most ceremony music is broken up into four parts: prelude, processional, ceremony, and recessional. Each of these sections has its own function and style; you should choose music that is suitable for each.

The Prelude

The prelude lasts from the time the guests start arriving until all of them are seated and the mother of the bride is ready to make her entrance. The options for music here are very broad; upbeat, slow, or a mixture of both. You want the prelude to establish a mood as well as entertain the guests while they wait. The end of the prelude, right before the processional, is usually a good time for a soloist or choir to sing a song (during the performance of which the mother of the bride would be seated).

The Processional

This is the music that accompanies the wedding party in their jaunt down the aisle. A traditional march helps to set the pace for nervous feet—and carry the spirit of the day toward the altar. When it's time for you to make that long trek down the aisle, you can walk to the same piece as the bridesmaids or to a piece chosen especially for you. Oftentimes the bride will walk to the same song as the bridesmaids, but played at a different tempo. Some processional favorites (and their composers) include:

"Waltz of the Flowers," Tchaikovsky
"Wedding March," Mendelssohn
"Bridal Chorus" (Here Comes the Bride), Wagner

"Trumpet Voluntary," Dupuis
"Trumpet Voluntary," Clarke
"Trumpet Tune," Purcell
"The Dance of the Sugar Plum Fairies," Tchaikovsky
"Ode to Joy," Beethoven
"The March," Tchaikovsky
"Ave Maria," Schubert
"The Austrian Wedding March" (traditional)

The Ceremony

Music played while the wedding ceremony itself takes place is called, oddly enough, ceremony music. The right music here can enhance the mood and emphasize the meaning of the marriage ceremony. Some ceremony music favorites (and their composers) include:

"My Tribute," Crouch
"The Lord's Prayer," Malotte
"Panis Angelicus," Franck
"Now Thank We All Our God," Bach
"Saviour Like a Shepherd Lead Us," Bradbury
"Cherish the Treasure," Mohr
"We've Only Just Begun," The Carpenters
"The Unity Candle Song," Sullivan
"The Bride's Prayer," Good
"The Wedding Prayer," Dunlap
"All I Ask of You," Norbet and Callahan
"Wherever You Go," Callahan
"The Wedding Song," Paul Stookey
"The Irish Wedding Song," traditional

The Recessional

This is your exit music. The song should be joyous and upbeat, reflecting your happiness at being joined for life to the man accompanying you back down the aisle. Some recessional favorites (and their composers) include:

"The Russian Dance," Tchaikovsky
"Trumpet Tune," Stanley
"Toccata Symphony V," Widor
"All Creatures of Our God and King," Williams
"Trumpet Fanfare (Rondeau)," Mouret
"Pomp and Circumstance," Elgar
"Praise, My Soul, the King of Heaven," Goss

The right music should complement and underscore the spirit of the marriage ceremony and may even help you get to the heart of the matter as you sit down to compose the vows that you will be speaking before your love, your family, and your friends.

Symbols of Love

To further personalize your wedding, you may choose to include a symbolic ceremony. Much like the ring exchange, the wine ceremony, and the unity candle–lighting ceremony are beautiful, albeit lesser-known, traditions that may add a great deal to your overall marriage ceremony. Likewise, you might want to consider following the custom of giving a flower from your bouquet to your mother and to your groom's mother as you walk up the aisle. Or, take your vows by candlelight and have the church bells ring as you are declared husband and wife. Check with your officiant before undertaking any unconventional plan of action, but always remember that this is your wedding and the sky is the limit!

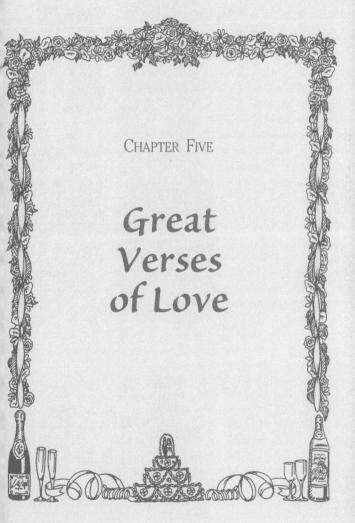

CHAPTER FIVE

Great
Verses
of Love

*I*n this chapter, you will find extracts from some of the greatest poems relating to love and marriage. You may wish to use one or more of these extracts, in conjunction with your answers to the brief questionnaire in Chapter 1, as a starting point for developing your own vows.

For example, you might decide to use the first extract that appears below, from Burr's "Certainty Enough," by having each partner recite two lines in sequence, and then conclude with something like this:

Bride: John, you are my constant star, the enduring point of light in my life. I give myself to you today for as long as I shall live on this earth.

Groom: Kathy, you are the constant source of love and support I have always longed for. I give myself to you today for as long as I shall live on this earth.

Alternatively, you may decide to use a quote as a supplementary reading during your wedding ceremony.

I am not sure that Earth is round
Nor that the sky is really blue.
The tale of why the apples fall
May or may not be true.
I do not know what makes the tides
Nor what tomorrow's world may do,
But I have certainty enough,
For I am sure of you.

—Amelia Josephine Burr

Drink to me only with thine eyes,
And I will pledge with mine;
Or leave a kiss but in the cup,
And I'll not look for wine.
The thirst that from the soul doth rise
Doth ask a drink divine;
But might I of Jove's nectar sup,
I would not change for thine.

—Ben Jonson

. . . come the wild weather, come sleet or come snow, We will stand by each other, however it blow.

—Simon Dach

We loved with a love that was more than a love.

—Edgar Allan Poe

. . . Love is not love Which alters when it alteration finds, Or bends with the remover to remove: O, no! it is an ever-fixed mark, That looks on tempests and is never shaken; It is the star to every wandering bark, Whose worth's unknown, although his height be taken.

—William Shakespeare

Love's mysteries in souls do grow, But yet the body is his book.

—John Donne

Our boat to the waves go free, By the bending tide, where the curled wave breaks, Like the track of the wind on the white snowflakes; Away, away! 'Tis a path o'er the sea.

—William Ellery Channing

Thou art the star that guides me Along life's changing sea; And whate'er fate betides me, This heart still turns to thee.

—George P. Morris

Now the rite is duly done, Now the word is spoken, And the spell has made us one Which may ne'er be broken.

—Winthrop Mackworth Praed

My fellow, my companion, held most dear, My soul, my other self, my inward friend.

—Mary Sidney Herbert

Flesh of my flesh, bone of my bone, I here, though there, yet both but one.

—Anne Bradstreet

Each shining light above us Has its own peculiar grace; But every light of heaven Is in my darling's face.

—John Hay

Those worlds, for which the conqueror sighs, For me would have no charms: My only world thy gentle eyes—My throne thy circling arms! Oh, yes, so well, so tenderly Thou'rt loved, adored by me, Whole realms of light and liberty Were worthless without thee.

—Thomas Moore

So they lovd as love in twain Had the essence but in one; Two distincts, division none . . .

—William Shakespeare

I think true love is never blind, But rather brings an added light, An inner vision quick to find The beauties hid from common sight. No soul can ever clearly see Another's highest, noblest part; Save through the sweet philosophy And loving wisdom of the heart.

—Phoebe Cary

Love is not getting, but giving; It is goodness, and honor, and peace and pure living.

—Henry Van Dyke

O, human love! thou spirit given On Earth, of all we hope in Heaven!

—Edgar Allan Poe

Love, all alike, no season knows, nor clime, Nor hours, days, months, which are the rags of time.

—John Donne

My bounty is as boundless as the sea. My love as deep; the more I give to thee, The more I have, for both are infinite.

—William Shakespeare

Were you the earth, dear Love, and I the skies, My love should shine on you like to the sun, And look upon you with ten thousand eyes Till heaven wax'd blind, and till the world were done.

—Joshua Sylvester

The violet loves a sunny bank, The cowslip loves the lea, The scarlet creeper loves the elm, But I love—thee.

The sunshine kisses mount and vale, The stars they kiss the sea, The west winds kiss the clover bloom, But I kiss—thee.

The oriole weds his mottled mate, The lilys bride o the bee; Heavens marriage ring is round the earth,—Shall I wed thee?

—Bayard Taylor

I wonder, by my troth, what thou and I did till we lov'd?

—John Donne

Two human loves make one divine.

—Elizabeth Barrett Browning

Young bride—a wreath for thee, Of sweet and gentle flowers; For wedded love was pure and free In Eden's happy bowers.

Young bride—a song for thee, A song of joyous measure, For thy cup of hope shall be Filled with honeyed pleasure. . . .

Young bride—a prayer for thee, That all thy hopes possessing, Thy soul may praise her God and he May crown thee with His blessing.

—Martin Farquhar Tupper

One half of me is yours, the other half yours—Mine own, I would say; but if mine, then yours, And so all yours!

—William Shakespeare

One heart's enough for me—One heart to love, adore—One heart's enough for me—O, who could wish for more? The birds that soar above, And sing their songs on high, Ask but for one to love, And therefore should not I?

One pair of eyes to gaze, One pair of sparkling blue, In which sweet love betrays Her form of fairest hue; One pair of glowing cheeks, Fresh as the rose and fair, Whose crimson blush bespeaks The health that's native there.

One pair of hands to twine Love's flowers fair and gay, And form a wreath divine, Which never can decay; And this is all I ask, One gentle form and fair—Beneath whose smiles to bask And learn love's sweetness there.

—Auguste Mignon

How much do I love thee? Go ask the deep sea How many rare gems In its coral caves be; Or ask the broad billows, That ceaselessly roar, How many bright sands Do they kiss on the shore?

—Mary Ashley Townsend

God hath made nothing single.

—Emily Dickinson

I'll love him more, more Than eer wife loved before, Be the days dark or bright.

—Jean Ingelow

Joy, gentle friends! Joy and fresh days of love Accompany your hearts!

—William Shakespeare

The fountains mingle with the river, And the rivers with the ocean; The winds of heaven mix forever, With a sweet emotion; Nothing in the world is single; All things by a law divine In one another's being mingle; Why not I with thine?

—Percy Bysshe Shelley

Love comforteth like sunshine after rain.

—William Shakespeare

Love to faults is always blind, Always is to joy inclin'd, Lawless, wing'd, and unconfin'd, And breaks all chains from every mind.

—William Blake

. . . true love is a durable fire, In the mind ever burning, Never sick, never old, never dead, From itself never turning.

—Sir Walter Raleigh

Love sought is good, but given unsought is better.

—William Shakespeare

Come live with me and be my love, And we will all the pleasures prove, That hills and valleys, dales and fields, Woods or craggy mountains yield.

—Christopher Marlowe

All love is sweet, Given or returned. Common as light is love, And its familiar voice wearies not ever. They who inspire it most are fortunate, As I am now; but those who feel it most Are happier still.

—Percy Bysshe Shelley

I know not if I know what true love is, But if I know, then, if I love not him, I know there is none other I can love.

—Alfred, Lord Tennyson

That Love is all there is, Is all we know of Love . . .

—Emily Dickinson

. . . Life with its myriad grasp Our yearning souls shall clasp By ceaseless love and still expectant wonder; In bonds that shall endure Indissolubly sure Till God in death shall part our paths asunder.

—Arthur Penrhyn Stanley

Such is my love, to thee I so belong, That for thy right myself will bear all wrong.

—William Shakespeare

. . . Rarely, rarely, comest thou, Spirit of Delight! I love all that thou lovest, Spirit of Delight The fresh Earth in new leaves dressed, And the starry night; Autumn evening and the morn When the golden mists are born. I love tranquil solitude, And such society as is quiet, wise and good; Between thee and me What difference? but thou dost possess The things I seek, not love them less.

—Percy Bysshe Shelley

If love were what the rose is, And I were like the leaf, Our lives would grow together In sad or singing weather, Blown fields or flowerful closes, Green pleasures or gray grief; If love were what the rose is, And I were like the leaf.

—Algernon Charles Swinburne

Love makes those young whom age doth chill, And whom he finds young, keeps young still.

—William Cartwright

Teacher, tender comrade, wife, A fellow-farer true through life.

—Robert Louis Stevenson

For thy sweet love rememberd such wealth brings, That then I scorn to change my state with kings.

—William Shakespeare

As dew beneath the wind of morning, As the sea which whirlwinds waken, As the bird's at thunder's warning, As aught mute yet deeply shaken, As one who feels an unseen spirit Is my heart when thine is near it.

—Percy Bysshe Shelley

Grow old along with me! The best is yet to be. The last of life, for which the first was made. Our times are in his hand Who saith, A whole I planned; Youth shows but half. Trust God; see all, nor be afraid!

—Robert Browning

Great Names in Romantic Writing

While this book has quotes enough to keep you non-speedreaders occupied for hours on end, there's no reason to restrict yourselves to the contents of these pages. The following writers have a lot to offer a bride and groom in the way of wedding vows and supplementary reading material.

Maya Angelou
Anne Bradstreet
Elizabeth Barrett Browning
Willa Cather
e.e. cummings
Emily Dickinson
John Donne
Ralph Waldo Emerson
Ben Johnson
John Keats
Anne Morrow Lindbergh
Henry Wadsworth Longfellow
John Milton
William Shakespeare
Percy Bysshe Shelley
Virgil
William Carlos Williams

How do I love thee? Let me count the ways. I love thee to the depth and breadth and height My soul can reach, when feeling out of sight For the ends of Being and ideal Grace. I love thee to the level of every day's Most quiet need, by sun and candle-light. I love thee freely, as men strive for Right; I love thee purely, as they turn from Praise. I love thee with the passion put to use In my old griefs, and with my childhood's faith. I love thee with a love I seemed to lose With my lost saints—I love thee with the breath, Smiles, tears of all my life!—and if God choose, I shall but love thee better after death.

—Elizabeth Barrett Browning

If ever two were one, then surely we.
If ever man were loved by wife, then thee.

—Anne Bradstreet

She walks in beauty, like the night
Of cloudless climes and starry skies;
And all that's best of dark and bright
Meet in her aspect and her eyes:
This mellowed to that tender light
Which heaven to gaudy day denies.

One shade the more, one ray the less,
Had half impaired the nameless grace
Which waves in every raven tress,
Or softly lightens o'er her face;
Where thoughts serenely sweet express
How pure, how dear their dwelling place.

—Lord Byron

Then Almitra spoke again and said, And what of
Marriage, Master?

And he answered saying:

You were born together, and together you shall be
forevermore.

You shall be together when the white wings of
death scatter your days.

Ay, you shall be together even in the silent memory
of God.

But let there be spaces in your togetherness,

And let the winds of the heavens dance between you.

Love one another, but make not a bond of love:

Let it rather be a moving sea between the shores of
your souls.

Fill each other's cup but drink not from one cup.

Give one another of your bread but eat not from the
same loaf.

Sing and dance together and be joyous, but let each
one of you be alone,

Even as the strings of a lute are alone though they
quiver with the same music.

Give your hearts, but not into each other's keeping.

For only the hand of Life can contain your hearts.

And stand together yet not too near together:

For the pillars of the temple stand apart,

And the oak tree and the cypress grow not in each
other's shadow.

—Kahlil Gibran

It is the heart and not the brain
That to the highest doth attain,
And he who followeth Love's behest
Far excelleth all the rest.

—Henry Wadsworth Longfellow

Fate, Time, Occasion, Chance, and Change? To these
All things are subject but eternal Love.

—Percy Bysshe Shelley

Life without love is like a tree without blossoms or fruit.

—Kahlil Gibran

Shall quips and sentences and these paper bullets
of the brain awe a man from the career of his
humor? No; the world must be peopled. When I said
I would die a bachelor, I did not think I should live
till I were married.

—William Shakespeare

Had I the heaven's embroidered cloths,
Enwrought with golden and silver light,
The blue and the dim of the dark cloths
Of night and light and the half-light,
I would spread the cloths under your feet:
But I being poor have only my dreams;
I have spread my dreams under your feet;
Tread softly, because you tread on my dreams.

—William Butler Yeats

I could not tell fact from fiction
Or if my dream was true
The only sure prediction
In this whole world was you . . .

—Maya Angelou

So, fall asleep love, loved by me. . . .
For I know love, I am loved by thee.

—Robert Browning

Hope is a thing with feathers
That perches in the soul
And sings a tune without words
And never stops at all.
And sweetest, in the gale, is heard
And sore must be the storm
That could abash the little bird
That keeps so many warm.
I've heard it in the chilliest land
And on the strangest sea
Yet, never, in extremity
It ask a crumb of me.

—Emily Dickinson

. . . let baser things devise
To lie in dust, but you shall live by fame;
My verse your virtues rare shall eternize,
And in the heavens write you glorious name:
Where, whenas Death shall all the world subdue,
Our love shall live, and later life renew.

—Edmund Spenser

. . . Alas,
We loved, sir—used to meet:
How sad and bad and mad it was—
But then, how it was sweet!
—Robert Browning

To see a world in a grain of sand
And a heaven in a wild flower
Hold infinity in the palm of your hand
And eternity in an hour.
—William Blake

Twice or thrice had I lov'd thee,
Before I knew thy face or name;
So in a voice, so in a shapeless flame
Angels affect us oft, and worshipp'd be;
Still when, to where thou wert, I came,
Some lovely glorious nothing I did see.
But since my soul, whose child love is,
Takes limbs of flesh, and else could nothing do,
More subtle than the parent is
Love must not be, but take a body too;
And therefore what thou wert, and who,
I bid Love ask, and now
That it assume thy body, I allow,
And fix itself in thy lip, eye, and brow.
—John Donne

Trust thou thy Love: if she be proud, is she not sweet?
Trust thou thy Love: if she be mute, is she not pure?
Lay thou thy soul full in her hands, low at her feet;
Fail, Sun and Breath!—yet, for thy peace,
She shall endure.
—John Ruskin

Somewhere I have never traveled,
Gladly beyond any experience,
Your eyes have their silence:
Something in me understands
The voice of your eyes is deeper than all.

—e. e. cummings

And if I can't be with you I would rather have a different face
And if I can't be near you I would rather be adrift
in space
And if the gods desert us I would burn this chapel
into flames
And if someone tries to hurt you I would put myself
in your place.

—Neil Finn

What is there in the vale of life
Half so delightful as a wife,
When friendship, love, and peace combine
To stamp the marriage bond divine?

—William Cowper

With thee conversing I forget all time,
All seasons and their change, all please alike.

—John Milton

. . ., I give you my hand!
I give you my love more precious than money,
I give you myself before preaching or law,
Will you give me yourself?

—Walt Whitman

Stone walls do not a prison make,
Nor iron bars a cage;
Minds innocent and quiet take
That for an hermitage;
If I have freedom in my love,
And in my soul am free,
Angels alone that soar above,
Enjoy such liberty.

—Richard Lovelace

Mine ear is much enamoured to thy note;
So is mine eye enthralled to thy shape;
And thy fair virtue's force perforce doth move me
On the first view to say, to swear, I love thee.

—William Shakespeare

There has fallen a splendid tear
From the passion-flower by the gate.
She is comming, my dove, my dear;
She is comming, my life, my fate;
The red rose cries, "She is near, she is near,"
And the white rose weeps, "She is late,"
The larkspur listens, "I hear, I hear,"
And the lily whispers, "I wait."

—Alfred, Lord Tennyson

Marriage is like a golden ring in a chain, whose beginning is a glance and whose ending is in eternity.

—Kahlil Gibran

There be none of Beauty's daughters
With a magic like Thee;
And like music on the waters
Is thy sweet voice to me.

—Lord Byron

Did my heart love 'til now? Forswear it
sight, for I never saw true beauty till tonight.

—William Shakespeare

your slightest look easily will unclose me
though i have closed myself as fingers,
you open always petal by petal myself as Spring opens
(touching skillfully, mysteriously) her first rose

—e. e. cummings

If thou must love me, let it be for nought
Except for love's sake only. Do not say,
I love her for her smile . . . her look . . .
    her way
Of speaking gently—for a trick of thought
That falls in well with mine, and, certes, brought
A sense of pleasant ease on such a day—
For these things in themselves, Beloved, may
Be changed, or change for thee—and love so wrought,
May be unwrought so. Neither love me for
Thine own dear pity's wiping my cheeks dry,—
A creature might forget to weep, who bore
Thy comfort long, and lose thy love thereby!
But love me for love's sake, that evermore
Thou mayst love on, through love's eternity.

—Elizabeth Barrett Browning

Pains of love be sweeter far than all other pleasures are.

—John Dryden

Love seeketh not Itself to please,
Nor for itself hath any care;
But for another gives its ease,
And builds a Heaven in Hells despair.

—William Blake

So dear I love him that with him, all deaths I could endure. Without him, live no life.

—William Shakespeare

All thoughts, all passions, all delights,
Whatever stirs this mortal frame,
All are but ministers of Love,
And feed his sacred flame.

—Samuel Taylor Coleridge

To me, fair friend, you never can be old
For as you were when first your eye I eyed,
Such seems your beauty still.

—William Shakespeare

What I do and what I dream include thee, as the wine must taste of its own grapes.

—Elizabeth Barrett Browning

But to see her was to love her, love but her, and love her forever.

—Robert Burns

Come when my heart is full of grief,
Or when my heart is merry;
Come with the falling of the leaf
Or with the redd'ning cherry.
—Paul Laurence Dunbar

'Tis sweet to know there is an eye will mark
Our coming, and look brighter when we come.
—Lord Byron

Look not in my eyes, for fear
They mirror true the sight I see,
And there you find your face too clear
And love it and be lost like me.
—A. E. Housman

Thou wert my joy in every spot,
My theme in every song.
And when I saw a stranger face
Where beauty held the claim,
I gave it like a secret grace
The being of thy name.
And all the charms of face or voice
Which I in others see
Are but the recollected choice
Of what I felt for thee.
—John Clare

My face in thine eye, thine in mine appears,
And true plain hearts do in the faces rest;
Where can we find two better hemispheres,
Without sharp north, without declining west?
Whatever dies, was not mix'd equally;
If our two loves be one, or, thou and I
Love so alike, that none do slacken, none can die.
—John Donne

What love is, if thou wouldst be taught,
Thy heart must teach alone—
Two souls with but a single thought,
Two hearts that beat as one.

—Friedrich Halm

Just because I loves you—
That's de reason why
Ma soul is full of color
Like da wings of a butterfly

Just because I loves you
That's de reason why
My heart's a fluttering aspen leaf
When you pass by.

—Langston Hughes

O my luve's like a red, red rose.
That's newly sprung in June;
O my luve's like a melodie
That's sweetly play'd in tune.
As fair art thou, my bonnie lass,
So deep in luve am I;
And I will love thee still, my Dear,
Till a' the seas gang dry.
Till a' the seas gang dry, my Dear,
And the rocks melt wi' the sun:
I will luve thee still, my Dear,
While the sands o' life shall run.
And fare thee weel my only Luve!
And fare thee weel a while!
And I will come again, my Luve,
Tho' it were ten thousand mile!

—Robert Burns

Hereafter in a better world than this,
I shall desire more love and knowledge of you.
—William Shakespeare

Fame, wealth and honor! what are you to Love?
—Alexander Pope

Were I as base as is the lowly plain,
And you, my Love, as high as heaven above,
Yet should the thoughts of me your humble swain
Ascend to heaven, in honour of my Love.
Were I as high as heaven above the plain,
And you, my Love, as humble and as low
As are the deepest bottoms of the main,
Whereso'er you were, with you my love should go.
Were you the earth, dear Love, and I the skies,
My love should shine on you like to the sun,
And look upon you with ten thousand eyes
Till heaven wax'd blind, and till the world were done.
Whereso'er I am, below, or else above you,
Whereso'er you are, my heart shall truly love you.
—Samuel Daniel

We cannot kindle when we will
The fire which in the heart resides,
The spirit bloweth and is still,
In mystery our soul abides.
—Matthew Arnold

I'll be as patient as a gentle stream
And make a pastime of each weary step,
Till the last step have brought me to my love;
And there I'll rest, as after much turmoil
A blessed soul doth in Elysium.
—William Shakespeare

Our State cannot be severed, we are one,
One Flesh; to lose thee were to lose my self.

—John Milton

So shall a friendship fill each heart
With perfume sweet as roses are,
That even though we be apart,
We'll scent the fragrance from afar.

—Georgia McCoy

My heart is ever at your service.

—William Shakespeare

Unable are the Loved to die
For Love is Immortality.

—Emily Dickinson

Now you will feel no rain,
For each of you will be shelter to the other.
Now you will feel no cold,
For each of you will be warmth to the other.
Now there is no more loneliness for you,
For each of you will be companion to the other.
Now you are two bodies,
But there is only one life before you.
Go now to your dwelling place,
To enter into the days of your togetherness.
And may your days be good, and long upon the earth.

—Apache Blessing

They do not love that do not show their love.

—William Shakespeare

If a thing loves, it is infinite.

—William Blake

Thou, Julia, thou hast metamorphos'd me;
Made me neglect my studies, lose my time,
War with good counsel, set the world at nought;
Made wit, with musing weak, heartsick with thought.

—William Shakespeare

Love will find a way through paths where wolves
fear to prey.

—Lord Byron

Doubt thou the stars are fire;
Doubt that the sun doth move:
Doubt truth to be a liar;
But never doubt, I love.

—William Shakespeare

O lyric Love, half angel and half bird
And all a wonder and a wild desire.

—Robert Browning

Earth holds no other like to thee,
Or if it doth, in vain for me.

—Lord Byron

Kisses are better fate than wisdom.

—e. e. cummings

That old miracle—Love-at-first-sight—
Needs no explanations. The heart reads aright
Its destiny sometimes.

—Owen Meredith

So dear I love him that with him, All deaths I could
　　endure.
Without him, live no life.

—William Shakespeare

They sin who tell us love can die;
With life all other passions fly,
All others are but vanity.

—Robert Southey

The face of all the world is changed, I think,
Since first I heard the footsteps of thy soul.

—Elizabeth Barrett Browning

I do not know what it is about you that closes and opens;
only something in me understands
the voice of your eyes is deeper than all roses.

—e.e. cummings

Love me, sweet, with all thou art,
Feeling, thinking, seeing,—
Love me in the lightest part,
Love me in full being.

—Elizabeth Barrett Browning

Upon that I kiss your hand, and I call you my queen.

—William Shakespeare

The sunlight claps the earth
And the moonbeams kiss the sea:
What are all these kissings worth
If thou kiss not me?

—Percy Bysshe Shelley

The first sound in the song of love!
Scarce more than silence is, and yet a sound.
Hands of invisible spirits touch the strings
Of the mysterious instrument, the soul,
And play the prelude of our fate.

—Henry Wadsworth Longfellow

Whoever lives true life will love true love.

—Elizabeth Barrett Browning

If music be the food of love, play on.

—William Shakespeare

I arise from dreams of thee
In the first sweet sleep of night,
when the winds are breathing low,
and the stars are shining bright.

—Percy Bysshe Shelley

There is not a breathing of the common wind that
will forget thee.

—William Wordsworth

The more of my poor heart you take
The larger grows my heart!
And, since some target I must show
For Cupid's cruel dart,
Oh, if mine own you deign to keep,
Then give me your sweet heart!

—Edmond Rostand

Once he drew with one long kiss
My whole soul through my lips,
As sunlight drinketh dew.

—Alfred, Lord Tennyson

To wait an Hour—is long—
If Love be just beyond—
To wait Eternity—is short—
If Love reward the end.

—Emily Dickinson

O, thou art fairer than the evening air clad in the
beauty of a thousand stars.

—Christopher Marlowe

I love thee, I love but thee
With a love that shall not die
Till the sun grows cold
And the stars grow old.

—William Shakespeare

Love! the surviving gift of Heaven,
The choicest sweet of Paradise,
In life's else bitter cup distilled.

—Thomas Campbell

Yes, Love indeed is light from heaven; A spark of
that immortal fire With angels shared, by Allah
given, To lift from earth our low desire.

—Lord Byron

What's earth with all its art, verse, music, worth
compared with love, found, gained and kept?

—Robert Browning

Long after moments of closeness have passed,
A part of you remains with me
And warms the places your hands have touched
And hastens my heart for your return.

—Robert Sexton

I sought for Love
But Love ran away from me.
I sought my Soul
But my Soul I couldn't see.
Then I sought You,
And I found all three.

—Unknown

CHAPTER SIX

Great
Thoughts

*I*n this chapter, you'll find some immortal prose observations on love. These extracts, too, may be helpful to you in developing your personalized wedding vows. A powerful quote can be an excellent way to begin your exchange of vows. Consider this example:

Bride: It's been said that Love is space and time—as measured by the heart.

Groom: Today, we begin a new life together, united by a love that has transcended distance, a love that will see us through the great journey of a lifetime, the journey through time.

Bride: We undertake that journey together as a new being, no longer two, but one.

Groom: Kathy, I offer you my heart, my life, and my faith; may our love be without measure through measureless time.

Bride: John, I offer you my heart, my life, and my faith; may our love be without measure through measureless time.

Love is a great beautifier.

—Louisa May Alcott

Of all the earthly music, that which reaches farthest into heaven is the beating of a truly loving heart.

—Henry Ward Beecher

Love is just friendship set to music.

—E. Joseph Crossman

It is a good thing to be rich and strong, but it is a better thing to be loved.

—Euripides

Those who love deeply never grow old. They may die of old age, but they die young.

—Benjamin Franklin

It isn't possible to love and to part.

—E. M. Forster

It was a violent case of mutual love at first sight, though neither party was aware of the fact . . .

—Mark Twain

Love is a game that two can play and both can win.

—Eva Gabor

Love is trembling happiness.

—Kahlil Gibran

We love because it is the only true adventure.

—Nikki Giovanni

No distance of place or lapse of time can lessen the love of those who are thoroughly persuaded of each other's worth.

—Robert Southey

Life is the flower for which love is the honey.

—Victor Hugo

To love one who loves you,
To admire one who admires you,
In a word, to be the idol of one's idol,
Is exceeding the limit of human joy;
It is stealing fire from heaven.

—Delphine de Girardin

Any couple's dream, wished with the same strength,
will come true.

—Susan Polis Schutz

In the arithmetic of love, one plus one equals everything, and two minus one equals nothing.

—Ninon de L'Enclos

What counts in making a happy marriage is not so much how compatible you are, but how you deal with incompatibility.

—George Levinger

Love endures only when the lovers love many things together and not merely each other.

—Walter Lippmann

In loving, you lean on someone to hold them up.

—Rod McKuen

We like someone because. We love someone although.

—Henri De Montherlant

Age does not protect you from love. But love, to some extent, protects you from age.

—Jeanne Moreau

Love is like a wild rose, beautiful and calm, but willing to draw blood in its defense.

—Mark A. Overby

Love is my decision to make your problem my problem.

—Robert Schuller

To love is to receive a glimpse of heaven.

—Karen Sunde

Love is the only gold.

—Alfred, Lord Tennyson

Love is life. All, everything that I understand, I understand only because I love.

—Leo Tolstoy

Where love is, there is God also.

—Leo Tolstoy

Where there is love there is life.

—Mahatma Gandhi

I like not only to be loved, but to be told I am loved.

—George Eliot

True love doesn't have a happy ending:
true love doesn't have an ending.

—Unknown

Love is an act of endless forgiveness,
a tender look which becomes a habit.

—Peter Ustinov

What I feel for you seems less of earth and more of a cloudless heaven.

—Victor Hugo

Love is being stupid together.

—Paul Valery

The power of a glance has been so much abused in love stories, that it has come to be disbelieved in. Few people dare now to say that two beings have fallen in love because they have looked at each other. Yet it is in this way that love begins, and in this way only. The rest is only the rest, and comes afterwards. Nothing is more real than these great shocks which two souls give each other in exchanging this spark.

—Victor Hugo

Let my love, like sunshine, surround you, and illuminate your freedom.

—Tagore

We are shaped and fashioned by what we love.

—Johann Wolfgang von Goethe

The hours I spend with you I look upon as sort of a perfumed garden, a dim twilight, and a fountain singing to it . . . you and you alone make me feel that I am alive. . . . Other men it is said have seen angels, but I have seen thee and thou art enough.

—George Moore

The way you let your hand rest in mine, my bewitching Sweetheart, fills me with happiness. It is the perfection of confiding love. Everything you do, the little unconscious things in particular, charms me and increases my sense of nearness to you, identification with you, till my heart is full to overflowing.

—Woodrow Wilson

Your words are my food, your breath my wine. You are everything to me.

—Sarah Bernhardt

I cannot exist without you—I am forgetful of every thing but seeing you again—my Life seems to stop there—I see no further. You have absorb'd me. I have a sensation at the present moment as though I were dissolving . . . I have been astonished that Men could die Martyrs for religion—I have shudder'd at it—I shudder no more—I could be martyr'd for my Religion—Love is my religion—I could die for that—I could die for you. My creed is Love and you are its only tenet—You have ravish'd me away by a Power I cannot resist.

—John Keats

Love gives itself; it is not bought.

—Henry Wadsworth Longfellow

In dreams and in love there are no impossibilities.

—Janos Arany

We are all born for love.
It is the principle of existence, and its only end.

—Benjamin Disraeli

Starting each day, I shall remind myself
to reach out and touch you, gently,
with my words, my eyes and with my fingers,
because I don't want to miss feeling you . . .
You know, I'm really convinced
that if you were to define love,
the only word big enough
to engulf it all would be "life"—
LOVE IS LIFE—in all its aspects . . .
And if you miss love, you miss life!

—Leo Buscaglia

It is only with the heart that one can see rightly.
What is essential is invisible to the eye.

—Antoine de Saint Exupery

For one human being to love another: that is perhaps the most difficult of our tasks; the ultimate, the
last test and proof, the work for which all other
work is but preparation.

—Rainer Maria Rilke

This is the miracle that happens every time to
those who really love; the more they give, the
more they possess.

—Rainer Maria Rilke

To love is to place our happiness in the happiness of another.

**—Gottfried Wilhelm
von Leibniz**

We seek the comfort of another. Someone to share the life we choose. Someone to help us through the never-ending attempt to understand ourselves, and in the end, someone to comfort us along the way.

—Marlin Finch Lupus

I have no desire to move mountains, construct monuments, or leave behind in my wake material evidence of my existence. But in the final recollection, if the essence of my being has caused a smile to have appeared upon your face or a touch of joy within your heart, then in living, I have made my mark.

—Thomas L. Odem Jr.

Love . . . has the greatest power, and is the source of all our happiness and harmony, and makes us friends with the gods who are above us, and with one another.

—Plato

If you find it in your heart to care for somebody else, you will have succeeded.

—Maya Angelou

One word frees us of all the weight and pain of life: that word is love.

—Sophocles

The secret of life is that all that we have and are is a gift of grace to be shared.

—Lloyd John Ogilve

You don't marry someone you can live with—you marry the person who you cannot live without.

—Unknown

I came alive when I started loving you.

—C. S. Lewis

Love's a thing that's never out of season.

—Barry Cornwall

Living is loving, and loving is living. One cannot exist without the other.

—Asha Sarma

True love doesn't consist of holding hands, it consists of holding hearts.

—O. A. Battista

I never knew how to worship until I knew how to love.

—Henry Ward Beecher

Love rules the court, the camp, the grove, And men below, and saints above: For love is heaven, and heaven is love.

—Walter Scott

Woe to the man whose heart has not learned while young to hope, to love—and to put its trust in life.

—Joseph Conrad

You don't love a woman because she is beautiful, but she is beautiful because you love her.

—Unknown

Where does the family start?
It starts with a young man
Falling in love with a girl
No superior alternative has yet been found!

—Winston Churchill

Love . . . includes fellowship in suffering, in joy, and in effort.

—Albert Schweitzer

Sometimes the heart sees what is invisible to the eye.

—H. Jackson Brown Jr.

You will find as you look back upon your life that the moments when you have truly lived are the moments when you have done things in the spirit of love.

—Henry Drummond

Listen to no one who tells you how to love.
Your love is like no other, and that is what makes it beautiful.
Your self is your divinity. . . .
Express yourself.

—Paul Williams

The greatest happiness of life is the conviction that we are loved—loved for ourselves, or rather, loved in spite of ourselves.

—Victor Hugo

To fall in love is easy, even to remain in it is not difficult; our human loneliness is cause enough. But it is a hard quest worth making to find a comrade through whose steady presence one becomes steadily the person one desires to be.

—Anna Louise Strong

The moment you have in your heart this extraordinary thing called love and feel the depth, the delight, the ecstasy of it, you will discover that for you the world is transformed.

—J. Krishnamurti

Love has nothing to do with what you are expecting to get, it's what you are expected to give—which is everything.

—Unknown

In love the paradox occurs that two beings become one and yet remain two.

—Erich Fromm

To fear love is to fear life, and those who fear life are already three parts dead.

—Bertrand Russell

Immature love says: "I love you because I need you." Mature love says: "I need you because I love you."

—Erich Fromm

The art of love . . . is largely the art of persistence.

—Albert Ellis

The best proof of love is trust.

—Joyce Brothers

The hardest of all is learning to be a well of affection, and not a fountain; to show them we love them not when we feel like it, but when they do.

—Nan Fairbrother

Love takes off masks that we fear we cannot live without and know we cannot live within.

—James Baldwin

Perfect love is rare indeed.

—Leo Buscaglia

The cure for all ills and wrongs, the cares, the sorrows and the crimes of humanity, all lie in the one word "love." It is the divine vitality that everywhere produces and restores life.

—Lydia Maria Child

Love is the immortal flow of energy that nourishes, extends and preserves. Its eternal goal is life.

—Smiley Blanton

We are all born for love. It is the principle of existence, and its only end.

—Benjamin Disraeli

Do all things with love.

—Og Mandino

Treasure the love you receive above all. It will survive long after your good health has vanished.

—Og Mandino

Absence is to love what wind is to fire; it extinguishes the small, it enkindles the great.

—Comte DeBussy-Rabutin

Nunc scio quit sit amor. (Latin)
Now I know what love is.

—Virgil

For it was not into my ear you whispered, but into my heart. It was not my lips you kissed, but my soul.

—Judy Garland

The joy that isn't shared dies young.

—Anne Sexton

Every man has his own destiny: the only imperative is to follow it, to accept it, no matter where it leads him.

—Henry Miller

No man is an island, entire of himself; every man is a piece of the continent.

—John Donne

When we are not in love too much, we are not in love enough.

—Comte DeBussy-Rabutin

The best and most beautiful things in the world cannot be seen or even touched they must be felt with the heart.

—Helen Keller

True love is the joy of life.

—John Clarke

This was love at first sight, love everlasting: a feeling unknown, unhoped for, unexpected—in so far as it could be a matter of conscious awareness; it took entire possession of him, and he understood, with joyous amazement, that this was for life.

—Thomas Mann

As love is a union, it knows no extremes of distance.

—Juana Ines de la Cruz

The love we give away is the only love we keep.

—Elbert Hubbard

When peoples care for you and cry for you, they can straighten out your soul.

—Langston Hughes

If I Lose Thy Love, I Lose My All.

—Alexander Pope

Love is the most universal, the most tremendous, and the most mysterious of the cosmic forces.

—Pierre Teilhard de Chardin

No matter what you've done for yourself or for humanity, if you can't look back on having given love and attention to your own family, what have you really accomplished?

—Lee Iacocca

Love has power to give in a moment what toil can scarcely reach in an age.

—Johann Wolfgang von Goethe

The love of God, unutterable and perfect, flows into a pure soul the way light rushes into a transparent object. The more love we receive, the more love we shine forth; so that, as we grow clear and open, the more complete the joy of loving is. And the more souls who resonate together, the greater the intensity of their love for, mirror like, each soul reflects the other.

—Dante

Both of us, of the love that makes us one.

—Christina Rossetti

Love possesses seven hundred wings, and each one extends from the highest heaven to the lowest earth.

—Djalal ad-Din Rumi

By the accident of fortune a man may rule the world for a time, but by virtue of love he may rule the world forever.

—Lao Tzu

We don't love qualities, we love persons; sometimes by reason of their defects as well as of their qualities.

—Jacques Jacques Maritain

Without love, the world itself would not survive.

—Lope de Vega

"Baby, You're the Only Dream I've Ever Had That's Come True."

—Robert Duvall (song title from *Tender Mercies* soundtrack)

True love is like ghosts, which everybody talks about and few have seen.

—François Duc de La Rochefoucauld

Love needs no logic for its mission.

—Charles A. Lindbergh

Thee lift me, and I'll lift thee, and we'll ascend together.

—Quaker proverb

The aim of love is to love: no more, and no less.

—Oscar Wilde

To love and win is the best thing. To love and lose, the next best.

—William M. Thackeray

Within you I lose myself
Without you I find myself
Wanting to be lost again.

—Unknown

The motto of chivalry is also the motto of wisdom;
to serve all, but love only one.

—Honoré de Balzac

When you love someone, you do not love them all
the time, in exactly the same way, from moment to
moment. It is an impossibility. It is even a lie to pretend to. And yet, this is exactly what most of us
demand. We have so little faith in the ebb and flow
of life, of love, of relationships. We leap at the flow
of time and resist in terror its ebb. We are afraid it
will never return. We insist on permanency, on
duration, on continuity; when the only continuity
possible in life, as in love, is in growth, in fluidity—
in freedom. The only real security is not in owning
or possessing, not in demanding or expecting, not
in hoping, even. Security in a relationship lies neither in looking back to what it was, nor forward to
what it might be, but living in the present and
accepting it as it is now. For relationships, too, must
be like islands. One must accept them for what they
are here and now, within their limits—islands sur-
rounded and interrupted by the sea, continuously
visited and abandoned by the tides.
One must accept the serenity of
the winged life, of ebb and
flow, of intermittency.

—Anne Morrow Lindbergh

Love is most nearly itself when here and now cease to matter.

—T. S. Eliot

The simple lack of her is more to me than others' presence.

—Edward Thomas

True love is the only heart disease that is best left to "run on"—the only affection of the heart for which there is no help, and none desired.

—Mark Twain

No one has ever known me as clearly as you. No one has ever shown me that love allows everything. Not pretty or safe or easy but something I never knew. Love within reason, that isn't love and I learned that from you.

—Stephen Sondheim

There isn't time—so brief is life—for bickerings, apologies, heartburnings, callings to account. There is only time for loving—and but an instant, so to speak, for that.

—Mark Twain

No cord or cable can draw so forcibly, or bind so fast, as love can do with a single thread.

—Robert Burton

The birthday of my life has come, my love has come to me.

—Christina Rossetti

I have led her home, my love, my only friend. There is none like her, none.

—Alfred, Lord Tennyson

The true beloveds of this world are in their lover's eyes lilacs opening, ship lights, school bells, a landscape, remembered conversations, friends, a child's Sunday, lost voices, one's favorite suit, autumn and all seasons.

—Truman Capote

Share your smile with everyone, but save your kiss for only one.

—Unknown

The love in your heart wasn't put there to stay. Love isn't until you give it away.

—Unknown

Shared joy is double joy. Shared sorrow is half sorrow.

—Swedish proverb

Do you want me to tell you something really subversive? Love is everything it's cracked up to be. That's why people are so cynical about it. . . . It really is worth fighting for, being brave for, risking everything for. And the trouble is, if you don't risk anything, you risk even more.

—Erica Jong

He who is in love is wise and is becoming wiser, sees newly every time he looks at the object beloved, drawing from it with his eyes and his mind those virtues which it possesses.

—Ralph Waldo Emerson

Love won't be tampered with, love won't go away. Push it to one side and it creeps to the other.

—Louise Erdrich

Love is a canvas furnished by nature and embroidered by imagination.

—Voltaire

Falling in love consists merely in uncorking the imagination and bottling the common-sense.

—Helen Rowland

If you live to be a hundred, I want to live to be a hundred minus one day so I never have to live without you.

—A. A. Milne

Love is love's reward.

—John Dryden

I call "crystallization" that action of the mind that discovers fresh perfections in its beloved at every turn of events.

—Stendhal

Life in abundance comes only through great love.

—Elbert Hubbard

Love is the active concern for the life and growth of that which we love.

—Erich Fromm

The first duty of love—is to listen.

—Paul Tillich

He has achieved success who has lived well, laughed often, and loved much.

—Bessie Stanley

It makes no difference how deeply seated may be the trouble, how hopeless the outlook, how muddled the tangle, how great the mistake. A sufficient realization of love will dissolve it all.

—Emmet Fox

I would love to spend all my time writing to you; I'd love to share with you all that goes through my mind, all that weighs on my heart, all that gives air to my soul; phantoms of art, dreams that would be so beautiful if they could come true.

—Luigi Pirandello

Keep love in your heart. A life without it is like a sunless garden when the flowers are dead. The consciousness of loving and being loved brings a warmth and richness to life that nothing else can bring.

—Oscar Wilde

The highest happiness on earth is marriage. Every man who is happily married is a successful man even if he has failed in everything else.

—William Lyon Phelps

Let us always meet each other with a smile, for the smile is the beginning of love.

—Mother Teresa

Love doesn't just sit there like a stone, it has to be made, like brick; remade all the time, made new.

—Ursula K. LeGuin

Love feels no burden, thinks nothing of trouble, attempts what is above its strength, pleads no excuse of impossibility; for it thinks all things lawful for itself, and all things possible.

—Thomas à Kempis

Love is a gift. You can't buy it, you can't find it, someone has to give it to you. Learn to be receptive of that gift.

—Kurt Langner

Sometimes your nearness takes my breath away; And all the things I want to say can find no voice. Then, in silence, I can only hope my eyes will speak my heart.

—Robert Sexton

My most brilliant achievement was my ability to be able to persuade my wife to marry me.

—Winston Churchill

As for me, to love you alone, to make you happy, to do nothing which would contradict your wishes, this is my destiny and the meaning of my life.

—Napoleon Bonaparte

Love is the energizing elixir of the universe, the cause and effect of all harmonies.

—Djalal ad-Din Rumi

Love that is hoarded moulds at last
Until we know some day
The only thing we ever have
Is what we give away.

—Louis Ginsberg

The most important things to do in the world are to get something to eat, something to drink and somebody to love you.

—Brendan Behan

A loving heart is the truest wisdom.

—Charles Dickens

In all the crowded universe There is but one stupendous word: Love. There is no tree that rears its crest, No fern or flower that cleaves the sod Nor bird that sings above its nest, But tries to speak this word of God.

—Josiah Gilbert Holland

Love is the expansion of two natures in such fashion that each includes the other, each is enriched by the other.

—Felix Adler

Love is the master key which opens the gates of happiness.

—Oliver Wendell Holmes

Love at its highest point—love, sublime, unique, invincible—leads us straight to the brink of the great abyss, for it speaks to us directly of the infinite and of eternity. It is eminently religious.

—Henri Amiel

Whatever our souls are made of, his and mine are the same.

—Emily Brontë

Let us have love and more love; a love that melts all opposition, a love that conquers all foes, a love that sweeps away all barriers, a love that aboundeth in charity, a large-heartedness, tolerance, forgiveness and noble striving, a love that triumphs over all obstacles.

—Abdul Baha

When one has once fully entered the realm of love, the world—no matter how imperfect—becomes rich and beautiful, it consists solely of opportunities for love.

—Søren Kierkegaard

Love is the poetry of the senses.

—Honoré de Balzac

Love is the crowning grace of humanity, the holiest right of the soul, the golden link which binds us to duty and truth, the redeeming principle that chiefly reconciles the heart of life, and is prophetic of eternal good.

—Petrarch

You are sanity in an insane world. You're reason where there isn't any reason. Reason to live.

—Madeleine L'Engle

Love, like Death, Levels all ranks, and lays the shepherd's crook Beside the scepter.

—Edward Bulwer-Lytton

Even memory is not necessary for love. There is a land of the living and a land of the dead and the bridge is love, the only survival, the only meaning.

—Thornton Wilder

Love isn't like a reservoir. You'll never drain it dry. It's much more like a natural spring. The longer and the farther it flows, the stronger and the deeper and the clearer it becomes.

—Eddie Cantor

An ounce of love is worth a pound of knowledge.

—John Wesley

Chains do not hold a marriage together. It is threads, hundreds of tiny threads, which sew people together through the years.

—Simone Signoret

Even if marriages are made in heaven, man has to be responsible for the maintenance.

—Kroehle

Come live in my heart and pay no rent.

—Samuel Lover

The one thing we can never get enough of is love. And the one thing we never give enough is love.

—Henry Miller

She missed him the days when some pretext served to take him away from her, just as one misses the sun on a cloudy day without having thought much about the sun when it was shining.

—Kate Chopin

There is only one path to Heaven. On Earth, we call it Love.

—Karen Goldman

A palace without affection is a poor hovel, and the meanest hut with love in it is a palace for the soul.

—Robert Green Ingersoll

We cannot all do great things, but we can do small things with great love.

—Mother Teresa

Love can make the summer fly, or a night seem like a lifetime.

—Andrew Lloyd Webber

When love has melted and mingled two beings into an angelic and sacred unity, the secret of life is found for them . . . they are then but the two wings of a single spirit. Love, soar!

—Victor Hugo

In love, one and one are one.

—Jean-Paul Sartre

Love demands all, and has a right to all.

—Ludwig van Beethoven

The person who tries to live alone will not succeed as a human being. His heart withers if it does not answer another heart. His mind shrinks away if he hears only the echoes of his own thoughts and finds no other inspiration.

—Pearl S. Buck

If love be timid it is not true.

—Spanish proverb

The most precious possession that ever comes to a man in this world is a woman's heart.

—Josiah G. Holland

Not love at first sight, but affection at first glance.

—Jim Kruta

We are each of us angels with only one wing. And we can only fly embracing each other.

—Luciano De Crescenzo

Married couples who love each other tell each other a thousand things without talking.

—Chinese proverb

In our life there is a single color, as on an artist's palette, which provides the meaning of life and art. It is the color of love.

—Marc Chagall

If we listened to our intellect, we'd never have a love affair. We'd never have a friendship. We'd never go into business, because we'd be cynical. Well, that's nonsense. You've got to jump off cliffs all the time and build your wings on the way down.

—Ray Bradbury

A successful marriage requires falling in love many times, always with the same person.

—Mignon McLaughlin

The soul that can speak through the eyes can also kiss with a gaze.

—Gustavo Adolfo Becquer

Take away love, and our earth is a tomb.

—Robert Browning

You call it madness, but I call it love.

—Don Byas

When you like someone, you like them in spite of their faults. When you love someone, you love them with their faults.

—Elizabeth Cameron

The way to love anything is to realize that it might be lost.

—G. K. Chesterton

Love is the expression of simplicity in emotion, the unattainable longing that comes so unexpectedly, with great subtlety and bliss.

—Luen Dao

The pain of love is the pain of being alive. It is a perpetual wound.

—Maureen Duffy

It is love, not reason, that is stronger than death.

—Thomas Mann

Beloved, all that is harsh and difficult I want for myself, and all that is gentle and sweet for thee.

—San Juan de la Cruz

The reduction of the universe to a single being, the expansion of a single being even to God, this is love.

—Victor Hugo

At the touch of love everyone becomes a poet.

—Plato

We do not judge the people we love.

—Jean Paul Sartre

A very small degree of hope is sufficient to cause the birth of love.

—Stendhal

There is no remedy for love but to love more.

—Henry David Thoreau

Love is a force more formidable than any other. It is invisible—it cannot be seen or measured, yet it is powerful enough to transform you in a moment, and offer you more joy than any material possession could.

—Barbara De Angelis

Not all of us have to possess earthshaking talent. Just common sense and love will do.

—Myrtle Auvil

For a crowd is not company; and faces are but a gallery of pictures; and talk but a tinkling cymbal, where there is no love.

—Francis Bacon

If it is your time, love will track you down like a cruise missile.

—Lynda Barry

The less you open your heart, the more your heart suffers.

—Deepak Chopra

I dreamed of a wedding of elaborate elegance; a church filled with flowers and friends. I asked him what kind of wedding he wished for; he said one that would make me his wife.

—Unknown

Love is the river of life in the world.

—Henry Ward Beecher

Love, like virtue, is its own reward.

—John Vanbrugh

Honor the ocean of love.

—George De Benneville

You can give without loving, but you cannot love without giving.

—Amy Carmichael

Love makes the wildest spirit tame, and the tamest spirit wild.

—Alexis Delp

That is the true season of love
When we believe that we alone can love
When no one has ever loved so before us
And no one will ever love in the same way after us.

—Johann Wolfgang von Goethe

For what is love itself, for the one we love best? An enfolding of immeasurable cares which yet are better than any joys outside our love.

—George Eliot

All mankind loves a lover.

—Ralph Waldo Emerson

The chemist who can extract from his heart's elements, compassion, respect, longing, patience, regret, surprise, and forgiveness and compound them into one can create that atom which is called love.

—Kahlil Gibran

Love is something eternal; the aspect may change, but not the essence.

—Vincent van Gogh

. . . she gets into the remotest recesses of my heart, and shines all through me.

—Nathaniel Hawthorne

Love is not blind—it sees more, not less. But because it sees more, it is willing to see less.

—Rabbi J. Gordon

[Being in love] is something like poetry. Certainly, you can analyze it and expound its various senses and intentions, but there is always something left over, mysteriously hovering between music and meaning.

—Muriel Spark

Love is a gift from God, and as we obey His laws and genuinely learn to serve others, we develop God's love in our lives. Love of God is the means of unlocking divine powers which help us to live worthily and to overcome the world.

—David B. Haight

Love is the final end of the world's history, the Amen of the universe.

—Novalis Hardenberg

We are most alive when we're in love.

—John Updike

It is mind, not body, that makes marriage last.

—Publilius Syrus

Time is too slow for those who wait; too swift for those who fear; too long for those who grieve; too short for those who rejoice. But for those who love, time is eternity.

—Lady Jane Fellowes

Two souls with but a single thought,
Two hearts that beat as one.

—Friedrich Halm

Let your love be like the misty rain, coming softly, but flooding the river.

—Madagascan proverb

A successful marriage is not a gift; it is an achievement.

—Ann Landers

Greet each day with your eyes open to beauty, your mind open to change, and your heart open to love.

—Paula Finn

For all the times I never said the things I should have, I thank you for all the times you understood.

—Flavia Weedn

True happiness is found in unselfish love, a love which increases in proportion as it is shared.

—Thomas Merton

For you see, each day I love you more, today more than yesterday and less than tomorrow.

—Rosemonde Gerard

Today I begin to understand what love must be, if it exists. . . . When we are parted, we each feel the lack of the other half of ourselves. We are incomplete like a book in two volumes of which the first has been lost. That is what I imagine love to be: incompleteness in absence.

—Goncourt

Love is the wisdom of the fool and the folly of the wise.

—Samuel Johnson

Love is the ultimate outlaw. It just won't adhere to any rules. The most any of us can do is sign on as its accomplice.

—Tom Robbins

My heart smiled when you kissed my lips. What a sweet surprise.

—Jan Arden

In vain have I struggled, it will not do. You must allow me to tell you how ardently I admire and love you.

—Jane Austen

Love never claims, it ever gives.

—Mahatma Gandhi

To love and be loved is to feel the sun from both sides.

—David Viscott

We live by admiration, hope and love.

—William Wordsworth

Love is, above all, the gift of oneself.

—Jean Anouilh

Remember that when you leave this earth, you can take with you nothing that you have received—only what you have given: a full heart enriched by honest service, love, sacrifice and courage.

—Francis of Assisi

Married love between man and woman is bigger than oaths guarded by right of nature.

—Aeschylus

When you make the sacrifice in marriage, you're sacrificing not to each other but to unity in a relationship.

—Joseph Campbell

Marriage is an Athenic weaving together of families, of two souls with their individual fates and destinies, of time and eternity—everyday life married to the timeless mysteries of the soul.

—Thomas Moore

Let men tremble to win the hand of a woman, unless they win along with it the utmost passion of her heart.

—Nathaniel Hawthorne

What a grand thing, to be loved! What a grander thing still, to love!

—Victor Hugo

Love is that condition in which the happiness of another person is essential to your own.

—Robert A. Heinlein

Love is the key that unlocks the door which leads to ultimate reality.

—Martin Luther King, Jr.

Love is a fruit in season at all times, and within reach of every hand.

—Mother Teresa

We attract hearts by qualities we display;
We retain them by qualities we possess.

—Jean Baptiste Anoino Suard

When two people relate to each other authentically and humanly, God is the electricity that surges between them.

—Martin Buber

All you need in the world is love and laughter. That's all anybody needs. To have love in one hand and laughter in the other.

—August Wilson

A supreme love, a motive that gives a sublime rhythm to a woman's life, and exalts habit into partnership with the soul's highest needs . . .

—George Eliot

Oh, what good will writing do? I want to put my hand out and touch you. I want to do for you and care for you. I want to be there when you're sick and when you're lonesome.

—Edith Wharton

I would rather have had
one breath of her hair
one touch of her mouth
than an eternity without it . . .

—from *The City of Angels*

All you need for happiness is a good gun, a good horse and a good wife.

—Daniel Boone

Oh, the comfort, the inexpressible comfort of feeling
    safe with a person;
having neither to weigh thoughts nor measure words,
but to pour them all out, chaff and grain together,
knowing that a faithful hand will take and sift them,
keep what is worth keeping,
and then, with the breath of kindness, blow the
    rest away.

—Dinah Maria Mulock Craik

One must learn to love and go through a good deal
of suffering to get to it . . . and the journey is always
towards the other soul . . .

—D. H. Lawrence

Heaven will be no heaven to me if I do not meet
my wife there.

—Andrew Jackson

Love doesn't make the world go 'round.
Love is what makes the ride worthwhile.

—Franklin P. Jones

One flower makes no garland.

—Romanian proverb

Well-married, a man is winged . . .

—Henry Ward Beecher

There is no more lovely, friendly and charming
relationship, communion or company than a good
marriage.

—Martin Luther

Love both gives and receives, and in giving it receives.

—Thomas Merton

Put away the book, the description, the tradition, the authority, and take the journey of self-discovery. Love, and don't be caught in opinions and ideas about what love is or should be. When you love, everything will come right. Love has its own action. Love, and you will know the blessings of it. Keep away from the authority who tells you what love is and what it is not. No authority knows and he who knows cannot tell. Love, and there is understanding.

—Krishnamurti

Love is . . . born with the pleasure of looking at each other, it is fed with the necessity of seeing each other, it is concluded with the impossibility of separation.

—José Marti Y Perez

I am, in every thought of my heart, yours.

—Woodrow Wilson

Love is not finding someone to live with, It's finding someone you can't live without.

—Rafael Ortiz

My dear, my better half.

—Sir Phillip Sidney

Who, being loved, is poor?

—Oscar Wilde

Love alone is capable of uniting living beings in such a way as to complete and fulfill them, for it alone takes them and joins them by what is deepest in themselves.

—Pierre Teilhard de Chardin

No words are necessary between two loving hearts.

—Unknown

You can transmute love, ignore it, or muddle it, but you can never pull it out of you.

—E. M. Forster

The most wonderful of all things in life, I believe, is the discovery of another human being with whom one's relationship has a glowing depth, beauty, and joy as the years increase. This inner progressiveness of love between two human beings is a most marvelous thing, it cannot be found by looking for it or by passionately wishing for it. It is sort of a Divine accident.

—Sir Hugh Walpole

There is only one happiness in life, to love and be loved.

—George Sand

Love conquers all things; let us too surrender to love.

—Virgil

To be able to say how much you love is to love but little.

—Petrarch

The heart has its reasons that reason does not know.
—Pascal

We see those we love in every sunrise and in every sunset, in every tree and in every flower.
—Unknown

Give all to love; obey thy heart.
—Ralph Waldo Emerson

To love deeply in one direction makes us more loving in all others.
—Madame Swetchine

Nobody ever measured, even poets, how much the heart can hold.
—Zelda Fitzgerald

I am two fools, I know, for loving, and for saying so in whining poetry.
—John Donne

Of all forms of caution, caution in love is perhaps the most fatal to true happiness.
—Bertrand Russell

If I had a flower for every time I thought of you, I could walk forever in my beautiful garden.
—Claudia Grandi

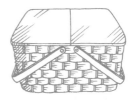

The one who desired to see the living God face to face, should not seek God in the empty ferment of the mind, but in human love.

—Fyodor Dostoevsky

We find rest in those we love, and we provide a resting place in ourselves for those who love us.

—Saint Bernard of Clairvaux

Love disregards manifest qualities and sees right through them down to the true essential value. Furthermore, love divines all the talents, the still dormant possibilities of the beloved, brings them to life, and thus increases his value.

—Oswald Schreiner

Love cannot be forced, love cannot be coaxed and teased. It comes out of Heaven, unasked and unsought.

—Pearl S. Buck

When the satisfaction or security of another person becomes as significant to one as is one's own satisfaction or security, then the state of love exists. So far as I know, under no other circumstances is a state of love present, regardless of the popular usage of the word.

—Harry Stack Sullivan

My love has given you my heart and my soul. They are yours to do with as you please. Please be careful with them.

—Robert Davis

What greater thing is there for two human souls than to feel that they are joined together to strengthen each other in all labour, to minister to each other in all sorrow, to share with each other in all gladness, to be one with each other in the silent unspoken memories?

—George Eliot

May love and laughter light your days, and warm your heart and home. May good and faithful friends be yours where ever you may roam. May peace and plenty bless your world with joy that long endures. May all life's passing seasons bring the best to you and yours.

—Irish blessing

May you always have . . .
Walls for the wind
A roof for the rain,
Tea beside the fire
Laughter to cheer you,
Those you love near you
And all your heart might desire!

—Irish blessing

Early marriage, long love.

—German proverb

To love is nothing. To be loved is something. To love and be loved is everything.

—Greek proverb

I have great hopes that we shall love each other all our lives as much as if we had never married at all.

—Lord Byron

True love is a durable fire in the mind ever burning.
—Sir Walter Raleigh

Love knows no rule.

—St. Jerome

Love is ever the beginning of knowledge, as fire is of light.

—Thomas Carlyle

Bitterness imprisons life; love releases it. Bitterness paralyzes life; love empowers it. Bitterness sours life; love sweetens it. Bitterness sickens life; love heals it. Bitterness blinds life; love anoints its eyes.

—Harry Emerson Fosdick

Oh, what a heaven is love!

—Thomas Dekker

Love is the only sane and satisfactory answer to the problem of human existence.

—Erich Fromm

Since love is the most delicate and total act of a soul, it will reflect the state and nature of the soul. If the individual is not sensitive, how can his love be sentient? If he is not profound, how can his love be deep? As one is, so is his love.

—José Ortega y Gasset

Love and you shall be loved.

—Ralph Waldo Emerson

The truth is that there is only one terminal dignity—love. And the story of a love is not important—what is important is that one is capable of love. It is perhaps the only glimpse we are permitted of eternity.

—Helen Hayes

Love is immortality.

—Plato

Love doesn't just sit there, like a stone; it has to be made, like bread, remade all the time, made new. Love keeps the cold out better than a cloak.

—Henry Wadsworth Longfellow

You will reciprocally promise love, loyalty, and matrimonial honesty. We only want for you this day that these words constitute the principle of your entire life; that with the help of divine grace you will observe these solemn vows that today, before God, you formulate.

—Pope John Paul II

Hail wedded love, mysterious law, true source of all humanity.

—John Milton

The web of marriage is made by propinquity, in the day to day living side by side, looking outward and working outward in the same direction. It is woven in space and in time of the substance of life itself.

—Anne Morrow Lindbergh

Only a life lived for another is worthwhile.

—Albert Einstein

This is one of the miracles of love: It gives . . . a power of seeing through its own enchantments and yet not being disenchanted.

—C. S. Lewis

How vast a memory has love!

—Alexander Pope

Love is enough, though the world be waning.

—William Morris

Love like ours can never die!

—Rudyard Kipling

There is no surprise more magical than the surprise of being loved: It is God's finger on man's shoulder.

—Charles Morgan

Love is that splendid triggering of human vitality . . . the supreme activity which nature affords anyone for going out of himself toward someone else.

—José Ortega y Gasset

Love vanquishes time. To lovers, a moment can be eternity, and eternity can be the tick of a clock.

—Mary Parrish

Love is not weakness. It is strong. Only the sacrament of marriage can contain it.

—Boris Pasternak

I would like to have engraved inside every wedding band: Be kind to one another. This is the Golden Rule of marriage and the secret of making love last through the years.

—Randolph Ray

Love is you, you and me.

—John Lennon

Love is an attempt to change a piece of a dream world into reality.

—Theodor Reik

Love does not consist of gazing at each other, but in looking outward together in the same direction.

—Antoine de Saint Exupery

Loving can cost a lot, but not loving always costs more, and those who fear to love often find that want of love is an emptiness that robs the joy from life.

—Merle Shain

When the wedding march sounds the resolute approach, the clock no longer ticks, it tolls the hour. . . . The figures in the aisle are no longer individuals. They symbolize the human race.

—Anne Morrow Lindbergh

Love is an energy which exists of itself. It is its own value.

—Thornton Wilder

My greatest good fortune in a life of brilliant experiences has been to find you, and to lead my life with you. I don't feel far away from you out here at all. I feel very near in my heart; and also I feel that the nearer I get to honour, the nearer I am to you.

—Winston Churchill, to his wife

Where there is great love there are always miracles.

—Willa Cather

Marriage is not a union merely between two creatures—it is a union between two spirits; and the intention of that bond is to perfect the nature of both.

—Frederick William Robertson

Love, indeed, lends a precious seeing to the eye, and hearing to the ear: all sights and sounds are glorified by the light of its presence.

—Frederick Saunders

Until I loved, I was a child.

—Charles Mackay

I wish to believe in immortality—I wish to live with you for ever.

—John Keats

When you love someone, you love the whole person, just as he or she is, and not as you would like them to be.

—Leo Tolstoy

Your embraces alone give life to my heart.
—Ancient Egyptian inscription

For those who love, time is eternity.
—Henry Van Dyke

An Ode to Friendship

It used to be that marriage and friendship were two separate and distinct entities. You had your wife or husband to tend after the kids or bring home the bacon, and then you had your friends who provided fun and camaraderie. The twain were never supposed to meet. Well, they can kiss that setup good-bye. As you and your fiancé probably know, friendship is the glue that will keep your marriage together just as it's kept your romance alive. Many of you probably began as friends and grew into a couple. Or you started dating and forged a friendship in the process. Either way, you might want to include a quote or a reading that will address the future of your beautiful friendship, and you'll find plenty from which to choose on the following pages.

A friend might well be reckoned the masterpiece of nature.

—Ralph Waldo Emerson

All love that has not friendship for its base is like a mansion built upon the sand.

—Ella Wheeler Wilcox

Everybody needs one essential friend.

—William Glasser

Life without a friend is death without a witness.

—Spanish proverb

What is a friend? One soul in two bodies.

—Aristotle

There's lots of things
With which I'm blessed,
Tho' my life's been both Sunny and Blue,
But of all my blessings,
This one's the best:
To have a friend like you.

In times of trouble
Friends will say,
"Just ask . . . I'll help you through it."
But you don't wait for me to ask,
You just get up and you do it!

And I can think
Of nothing in life
That I could more wisely do,
Than know a friend,
And be a friend,
And love a friend . . . like you.

—Unknown

Two may talk together under the same roof for many years, yet never really meet; and two others at first speech are old friends.

—Mary Catherwood

A single rose can be my garden . . . a single friend, my world.

—Leo Buscaglia

Plant a seed of friendship; reap a bouquet of happiness.

—Lois L. Kaufman

It takes a long time to grow an old friend.

—John Leonard

One of the most beautiful qualities of true friendship is to understand and to be understood.

—Seneca

Wishing to be friends is quick work,
but friendship is a slow ripening fruit.

—Aristotle

Friends are not necessary to live. They do, however, make life worth living.

—C. S. Lewis

Remember, the greatest gift is not found in a store nor under a tree, but in the hearts of true friends.

—Cindy Lew

A true friend unbosoms freely, advises justly, assists readily, adventures boldly, takes all patiently, defends courageously, and continues a friend unchangeably.

—William Penn

There are high spots in all of our lives,
and most of them come about
through encouragement from someone else.

—George Adams

Friends will not only live in harmony, but in melody.

—Henry David Thoreau

Our most intimate friend is not he to whom we show the worst, but the best, of our nature.

—Nathaniel Hawthorne

If instead of a gem, or even a flower,
we should cast the gift of a loving thought into the
    heart of a friend,
that would be giving as the angels give.

—George Macdonald

To bear each other's burdens, never to ask each other for anything inconsistent with virtue and rectitude, and not only to serve and love but also to respect each other.

—Cicero

Let us be grateful to people who make us happy; they are the charming gardeners who make our souls blossom.

—Marcel Proust

Friendship is a strong and habitual inclination in two persons to promote the good and happiness of one another.

—Eustace Budgell

Friendship improves happiness and abates misery, by the doubling of our joy and the dividing of our grief.

—Cicero

The soul needs friendship, the heart needs love.

—Ed Habib

We are all travelers in the wilderness of this world, and the best that we can find in our travels is an honest friend.

—Robert Louis Stevenson

Friends are as companions on a journey, who ought to aid each other to persevere in the road to a happier life.

—Pythagoras

Friends . . .
They cherish one another's hopes.
They are kind to one another's dreams.

—Henry David Thoreau

A friend is one who knows you and loves you just the same.

—Elbert Hubbard

The glory of friendship is not the outstretched hand,
nor the kindly smile nor the joy of companionship;
it is the spiritual inspiration that comes to one when
    he discovers
that someone else believes in him and is willing to
    trust him.

—Ralph Waldo Emerson

A friend hears the song of my heart and sings it to
me when my memory fails.

—Unknown

Friendship is
the breathing rose,
With sweets in every fold.

—Ralph Waldo Emerson

A blessed thing it is for any man or woman to have
a friend, one human soul whom we can trust utterly,
who knows the best and worst of us, and who loves
us in spite of all our faults.

—Charles Kingsley

What do we live for,
if not to make life less difficult
for each other?

—George Eliot

In everyone's life, at some time, our inner fire goes out.
It is then burst into flame by an encounter with
    another human being.
We should all be thankful for those people who
    rekindle the inner spirit.

—Albert Schweitzer

Once I knew only darkness and stillness . . .
my life was without past or future . . .
but a little word from the fingers of another
fell into my hand that clutched at emptiness,
and my heart leaped to the rapture of living.

—Helen Keller

True friendship is a plant of slow growth,
and must undergo and withstand the shocks
    of adversity,
before it is entitled to the appellation.

—George Washington

Be slow to fall into friendship; but when thou art in,
continue firm and constant.

—Socrates

Many a time from a bad beginning great friendships
have sprung up.

—Terence

To know someone, here
or there, with whom you
feel there is understanding
in spite of distances or
thoughts unexpressed—
that can make of this
earth a garden.

**—Johann Wolfgang
von Goethe**

Love is friendship that has caught fire.

—Ann Landers

Who much to be prized and esteemed is a friend,
On whom we may always with safety depend;
Our joys when extended will always increase,
And griefs when divided are hushed into peace.

—Aesop

Best friend, my wellspring in the wilderness!

—George Eliot

[Friendship] redoubleth joys and cutteth griefs in halves. For there is no man that imparteth his joys to his friend, but he joyeth the more; and no man that imparteth his griefs to his friend, but he griefeth the less.

—Francis Bacon

Friendship that flows from the heart cannot be frozen by adversity, as the water that flows from the spring cannot congeal in winter.

—James Fenimore Cooper

Blessed is the influence of one true, loving human soul on another.

—George Eliot

Each friend represents a world in us, a world possibly not born until they arrive, and it is only by this meeting that a new world is born.

—Anaïs Nin

A friend is one that knows you as you are, understands where you have been, accepts what you have become, and still, gently allows you to grow.

—William Shakespeare

Treasure each other in the recognition that we do not know how long we shall have each other.

—Joshua Loth Liebman

Don't walk in front of me, I may not follow.
Don't walk behind me, I may not lead.
Just walk beside me and be my friend.

—Albert Camus

The greatest sweetener of human life is Friendship. To raise this to the highest pitch of enjoyment, is a secret which but few discover.

—Joseph Addison

A friend is someone you want to be around when you feel like being by yourself.

—Burrow

Love is friendship plus sex and minus reason.

—Mason Cooley

A friend is someone who, upon seeing another friend in immense pain, would rather be the one experiencing the pain than to have to watch their friend suffer.

—Amanda Gier

Sometimes, when one person is missing, the whole world seems depopulated.

—Alphonse de Lamartine

True friends don't spend time gazing into each other's eyes. They may show great tenderness towards each other, but they face in the same direction—toward common projects, goals—above all, towards a common Lord.

—C. S. Lewis

To feel the love of people whom we love is a fire that feeds our life.

—Pablo Neruda

Friendship is . . . the sort of love one can imagine between angels.

—C. S. Lewis

Hold a true friend with both hands.

—Nigerian proverb

My best friend is the one who brings out the best in me.

—Henry Ford

Friendship's the wine of life.

—Edward Young

A friend is, as it were, a second self.

—Cicero

Grief can take care of itself, but to get the full value out of joy, you must have someone to divide it with.

—Mark Twain

I could do without many things with no hardship— you are not one of them.

—Ashleigh Brilliant

Continue to be my friend, as you will always find me yours.

—Ludwig van Beethoven

Scriptural Passages You May Want to Incorporate

What follows is a selection of passages appropriate for weddings from holy writings in a number of faiths. Even if yours is a civil or secular affair, you may decide that it is appropriate to incorporate one of the following scriptural passages into your memory.

If your ceremony is to take place within the context of an established religious tradition, be sure to review your choice of scripture selection with your officiant. Your tradition may require that you follow certain guidelines in choosing verses.

> And God blessed them, and God said to them, Be fruitful and multiply, and fill the earth and subdue it.
> **—Genesis 1:28**

> How much better is thy love than wine!
> **—Song of Solomon 4:10**

> When the one man loves the one woman
> and the one woman loves the one man,
> the very angels desert heaven and sit
> in that house and sing for joy.
> **—Braham-Sutra**

> And the Lord God said, It is not good that the man should be alone; I will make him a help meet for him. And out of the ground, the Lord God formed every beast of the field, and every fowl of the air; and brought them unto Adam to see what he would call them: and whatsoever Adam

called every living creature, that was the name thereof. And Adam gave names to all cattle, and to the fowl of the air, and to every beast of the field; but for Adam there was not found a help meet for him. And the Lord caused a deep sleep to fall upon Adam, and he slept: and he took one of his ribs, and closed up the flesh instead thereof; and the rib, which the Lord God had taken from the man, made he a woman, and brought her unto the man. And Adam said, This is now bone of my bones, and flesh of my flesh: she shall be called Woman, because she was taken out of Man. Therefore shall a man leave his father and his mother, and shall cleave unto his wife; and they shall be one flesh.

—Genesis 2:18–24

From the beginning of creation God made them male and female. For this cause shall a man leave his father and mother, and cleave to his wife; and they twain shall be one flesh: so then they are no more twain, but one flesh. What therefore God hath joined together, let not man put asunder.

—Mark 10:6–9

As the Father hath loved me, so have I loved you: continue ye in my love. If ye keep my commandments, ye shall abide in love; even as I have kept my Father's commandments, and abide in his love. These things have I spoken unto you, that my joy might remain in you, and that your joy might be full. This is my commandment: that ye love one another as I have loved you.

—John 15:9–12

The moral man will find the moral law beginning in the relation between husband and wife, but ending only in the vast reaches of the universe.

—Confucius

Walk in love, as Christ also hath loved us, and hath given himself for us as an offering and a sacrifice to God for a sweet-smelling savor.

—Ephesians 5:2

Blessed is every one that feareth the Lord; that walketh in his ways. For thou shalt eat the labor of thine hands; happy shalt thou be, and it shall be well with thee. Thy wife shall be as a fruitful vine by the sides of thine house, thy children like olive plants around thy table. Behold, that thus shall the man be blessed that feareth the Lord.

—Psalm 128: 1–4

He brought me to the banqueting house, and his banner over me was love.

—Song of Solomon 2:4

I am He, you are She; I am Song, you are Verse; I am Heaven, you are Earth. Together shall we dwell here, becoming parents of children.

—Atharva Veda

Whither thou goest, I will go; and where thou lodgest, I will lodge; thy people shall be my people, and thy God, my God. Where thou diest, will I die, and there will I be buried.

—Ruth 1:16–17

Many waters cannot quench love, neither can the floods drown it.

—Song of Solomon 8:7

Love is patient; love is kind and envies no one. Love is never boastful, nor conceited, nor rude; never selfish, not quick to take offense. Love keeps no score of wrongs; does not gloat over other men's sins, but delights in the truth. There is nothing love cannot face; there is no limit to its faith, its hope, and its endurance.

—I Corinthians 13:4–7

When two people are at one in their inmost hearts, they shatter even the strength of iron or of bronze.

—The I Ching

Blessed art thou, O Lord, King of the Universe, who created mirth and joy, bridegroom and bride, gladness, jubilation, dancing, and delight, love and brotherhood, peace and fellowship. Quickly, O, Lord our God, may 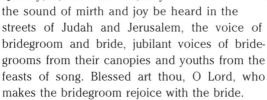 the sound of mirth and joy be heard in the streets of Judah and Jerusalem, the voice of bridegroom and bride, jubilant voices of bridegrooms from their canopies and youths from the feasts of song. Blessed art thou, O Lord, who makes the bridegroom rejoice with the bride.

—The Talmud (Ketubot 8a)

My beloved spake, and said unto me, Rise up, my love, my fair one, and come away.

—Song of Solomon 2:10

Sweet be the glances we exchange, our faces showing true concord. Enshrine me in thy heart, and let a single spirit dwell within us.

—Atharva Veda

Make a joyful noise unto the Lord, all ye lands. Serve the Lord with gladness: come before his presence with singing. Know ye that the Lord he is God: it is he that hath made us, and not we ourselves; we are his people, and the sheep of his pasture. Enter into his gates with thanksgiving, and into his courts with praise: be thankful unto him, and bless his name. For the Lord is good, his mercy is everlasting; and his truth endureth to all generations.

—Psalm 100

Only the complete person can love.

—Confucius

Husbands ought to love their wives as their own bodies. He who loves his wife loves himself.

—Ephesians 5:25–26

Set me as a seal upon thy heart, as a seal upon thine arm: for love is strong as death.

—The Bible

Love . . . binds everything together in perfect harmony.

—Colossians 3:14

When love is strong, a man and woman can make their bed on a sword's blade. When love grows weak, a bed of 60 cubits is not large enough.

—The Talmud

I have found the one whom my soul loves.

—Song of Solomon 3:4

There is no fear in love, but perfect love casts out fear.

—I John 4:18

He who does not love does not know God; for God is love.

—I John 4:8

Two are better than one because they have a good reward for their labor. For if they fall, one will lift up his companion. But woe to him who is alone when he falls, for he has no one to help lift him up.

—Ecclesiastes 4:9–10

May the love you share be as timeless as the tides and as deep as the sea.

—I Corinthians 13

When a man is newly married, he shall not go out with the army or be charged with any business; he shall be free at home one year, to be happy with his wife whom he has taken.

—Deuteronomy 24:5

Let him kiss me with the kisses of his mouth: for thy love is better than wine.

—Song of Solomon 1:2

And now abide faith, hope, love, these three; but the greatest of these is love.

—I Corinthians 13:13

Let us not love in word, neither in tongue; but in deed and in truth.

—I John 3:18

True love is the absence of fear.

—I John 4:18

As the lily among thorns, so is my love among the daughters. As the apple tree among the trees of the wood, so is my beloved among the sons. I sat down under his shadow with great delight, and his fruit was sweet to my taste.

—Song of Solomon 2:2–3

I may be able to speak the languages of human beings and even of angels, but if I have no love, my speech is no more than a noisy gong or a clanging bell. I may have the gift of inspired preaching; I may have all knowledge and understand all secrets; I may have the faith needed to move mountains—but if I have no love, I am nothing. I may give away everything I have, and even give up my body to be burned—but if I have no love, this does me no good.

—I Corinthians 13:1–13

Above all else, guard thy heart for it is the well-spring of life.

—Proverbs 4:23

Come let us take our fill of love until the morning: let us solace ourselves with love.

—Proverbs 7:18

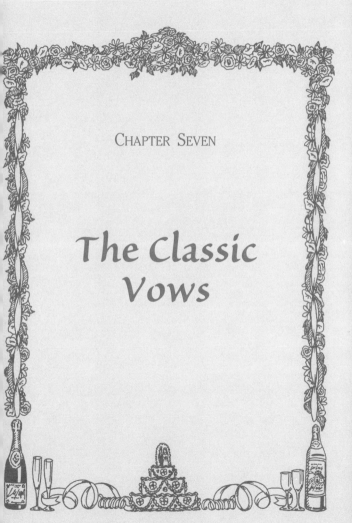

CHAPTER SEVEN

The Classic Vows

Whether you are marrying in a secular ceremony or a religious one, you may want to review some of the most popular accepted vows. You may decide to use what follows as a framework for use in developing your own vows, whether or not you belong to the tradition in which the vow was developed.

I, (name), take thee, (name), to be my wedded (husband/wife), to have and to hold from this day forward, for better, for worse, for richer, for poorer, in sickness and in health, to love and to cherish, till death do we part, according to God's holy ordinance; thereto I plight thee my troth.

—The Book of Common Prayer

I, (name), take you, (name), to be my (husband/wife), and these things I promise you: I will be faithful to you and honest with you; I will respect, trust, help, and care for you; I will share my life with you; I will forgive you as we have been forgiven; and I will try with you better to understand ourselves, the world, and God; through the best and the worst of what is to come as long as we live.

—Suggested Lutheran marriage vow

Groom: In the name of God, I, (name), take you, (name), to be my wife, to have and to hold from this day forward, for better for worse, for richer for poorer, in sickness and in health, to love and to cherish, until we are parted by death. This is my solemn vow.

Bride: In the name of God, I, (name), take you, (name), to be my husband, to have and to hold from this day forward, for better for worse, for richer for poorer, in sickness and in health, to love and to cherish, until we are parted by death. This is my solemn vow.

—Episcopal Church exchange of vows

I, (name), take you, (name), to be my (husband/wife). I promise to be true to you in good times and in bad, in sickness and in health. I will love you and honor you all the days of my life.

I, (name), take you, (name), for my lawful (husband/wife), to have and to hold, from this day forward, for better, for worse, for richer, for poorer, in sickness and in health, until death do us part.

—U.S. alternatives for vows within the Roman Catholic tradition. (If it seems preferable for pastoral reasons, the priest may obtain consent from the couple by asking questions based on the above and receiving the responses I do from each partner.)

Officiant: Christ calls you into union with him and with one another. I ask you now in the presence of God and this congregation to declare your intent. Will you have this man to be your husband, to live together in a holy marriage? Will you love him, comfort him, honor and keep him in sickness and in health, and forsaking all other, be faithful to him as long as you both shall live?
Bride: I will.
Officiant: Will you have this woman to be your wife, to live together in a holy marriage? Will you love her, comfort her, honor and keep her in sickness and in health, and forsaking all other, be faithful to her as long as you both shall live?
Groom: I will.

—United Methodist Church declaration of consent

Behold, you are consecrated unto me with this ring, according to the law of Moses and of Israel.
—In Jewish wedding ceremonies, the groom's words to the bride as he places a wedding ring on her finger after both have drunk from a cup of blessed wine. (Note: Betrothal rituals within the Jewish tradition vary widely; the ceremony is usually quite intricate, featuring a number of prayers and blessings.)

I pledge, in honesty and sincerity, to be for you a helpful/obedient and faithful husband/wife.
—Muslim wedding vows (Note: The majority of Muslim couples do not exchange spoken vows, instead they listen to the cleric speak about the responsibilities of marriage and the Muslim faith, and then agree to become husband and wife.)

Let us take the fourth step, to acquire knowledge, happiness, and harmony by mutual love and trust. . . . Finally, let us take the seventh step and become true companions and remain lifelong partners by this wedlock.
—A sample of the pledges that Hindu couples make to each other during traditional Hindu weddings.

In the presence of God and these our friends I, (name), take thee, (name), to be my (husband/wife), promising with Divine assistance to be unto thee a loving and faithful (husband/wife) so long as we both shall live.
—Traditional Quaker vows

I, (name), take you, (name), as my wedded (wife/husband) and I promise you love, honor, and respect; to be faithful to you, and not to forsake you until death do us part. So help me God, one in the Holy Trinity, and all the Saints.

—Russian Orthodox wedding vow

(Name), I take you to be my lawfully wedded (husband/wife). Before these witnesses I vow to love you and care for you for as long as we both shall live. I take you with your faults and your strengths, as I offer myself to you with my faults and my strengths. I will help you when you need help, and turn to you when I need help. I choose you as the person with whom I will spend my life.

—Exchange of vows in standard civil ceremony (one of many variations)

CHAPTER EIGHT

Nontraditional Vows to Use or Adapt

*I*n this part of the book, you will find a number of nontraditional wedding vows meant to be recited by each partner. If you wish, you may use them as written—but if you feel that a measure of personalization is in order, you should certainly feel free to adapt, amend, expand, or delete whatever you see fit. After all, it's your big day!

Today, (name), I join my life to yours, not merely as your (wife/husband), but as your friend, your lover, and your confidant. Let me be the shoulder you lean on, the rock on which you rest, the companion of your life. With you I will walk my path from this day forward.

(Name), with free and unconstrained soul, I give you all I am and all I am to become. Take this ring, and with it my promise of faith, patience, and love, for the rest of my life.

I come here today, (name), to join my life to yours before this company. In their presence I pledge to be true to you, to respect you, and to grow with you through the years. Time may pass, fortune may smile, trials may come; no matter what we may encounter together, I vow here that this love will be my only love. I will make my home in your heart from this day forward.

What have I to give you, (name)? A ring, and more than a ring: the promise to take you as my only love from this day forward, to stand by your side, to listen when you speak, to comfort you when you cry, and to join your laughter with my own. Take this ring, and be my (husband/wife).

As freely, (name), as God has given me life, I join my life with yours. Wherever you go, I will go; whatever you face, I will face. For good or ill, in happiness or sadness, come riches or poverty, I take you as my (husband/wife), and will give myself to no other.

(Name), you are the one with whom I can share all that I am. Take this ring as a token of my love. Let us live our lives together from this day forward.

To marry the person you have set your heart upon is a joy unparalleled in human life. (Name), take this ring as a sign of my faith and my commitment to our love, and share this joy with me today.

Yesterday, I was separate; today, I join my life with yours. Without hesitation and with full confidence in the step I am taking, I, (name), offer myself to you, (name), as your husband/wife.

I used to be afraid of falling in love, of giving my heart away. How could I trust a (man/woman) to love me, to give to me all that I wanted to give to (him/her)? (Name), when I met you, I realized how much we could share together. You have renewed my life; today I join that life with yours.

(Name), the words I say to you now are ones I have waited a lifetime to utter, ones I say in love and in confidence. I see in you a strong, growing partner, the person with whom I wish to share my life. I offer you all the days before me, no matter what may come our way. I freely take you as my (husband/wife). Take this ring as a sign of my commitment.

(Name), I promise to stand by you, to be there when you need me, and to share the happiness and sadness of my life with you. If the secret of life is to enjoy the passage of time, then let us share our time together from this day forward.

Love is something to express, not something to define. (Name), I take today as the opportunity for the fullest expression of my love for you. Here, before these honored guests, I commit to share my life with you as your (husband/wife).

I have only one way, and that is with you. (Name), take this ring, and with it, my love from this day forward. Today I become your (husband/wife).

A ceremony is for a day; a marriage is for a lifetime. Today, I join my life with yours for as long as I shall live on this earth, forsaking all others. (Name), I freely offer myself to you as your (husband/wife).

Come health, happiness, and prosperity, I will stand with you; come illness, trouble, or poverty, I will stand with you. Take this ring, (name), as a sign of my love and commitment.

Two flames, one light. (Name), I offer you this ring as a sign of life, and myself as your (husband/wife). Let us walk together always, and let us always walk toward the light.

I came to this place today as a (man/woman) standing alone; I will walk from it by your side. Today I cross the threshold with you and enter into a new and lasting lifetime commitment. (Name), I commit myself to you as your (husband/wife).

(Name), take this ring as a sign of my love and fidelity. I vow before this company to share my life with you from today onward.

(Name), today we begin our new life together. Let us assume our new roles as marriage partners with love, understanding, trust, and mutual fidelity for as long as we both shall live.

Today, a day of music and celebration, I pledge to share my life with you. Whether the days that come are happy or sad, I will live them with you. (Name), I give myself to you as your (husband/wife).

Love has given us wings, and our journey begins today. (Name), wherever the wind may carry me, I will stay by your side as your (husband/wife). Take this ring as a sign of my love.

Where there has been cold, you have brought warmth; where my life was dark, you have brought light. (Name), I pledge before this assembled company to be your (husband/wife) from this day forward. Let us make of our two lives one life, and let us always honor and respect each other.

Love is to be cherished when we find it in life, and I cherish it in you. (Name), let us build a life together. I give myself to you as your (husband/wife), and I pledge here to cherish for all of my days the love we celebrate today.

(Name), I am most myself when I am with you. As we begin our life together today, I pledge to respect your unique talents and abilities, and to stand by your side as we grow together over the years. Let us join our lives together and find ourselves anew each day.

When I become your (husband/wife) today, I enter into a new phase of life, and I do so with joy and with anticipation of the life we will share together. I pledge before this honored gathering of friends and family always to honor and respect our love. (Name), let us be as one.

Snow falls, but in time it melts; the sun shines, but in time night falls. Through passing time and the passing of life, we find meaning only in bringing joy to another. (Name), join me in this life, and let us pass winter and summer, night and day together, from this day forward.

(Name,) I join my life with yours today without hesitation and with an open and trusting heart. Whatever we may encounter, let us encounter it together. Take this ring, and with it my commitment to be the best (husband/wife) I can be.

(Name), our miracle lies in the path we have chosen together. I enter into this marriage with you knowing that the true magic of love is not to avoid changes, but to navigate them successfully. Let us commit to the miracle of making each day work—together.

(Name), I begin my life with you today knowing that we have developed a trust and a commitment that is strong enough to support both good times and bad times. No matter what may come, I pledge to stand by you. May our love deepen and grow with the years, and may we always share in the changes of life with flexibility and respect for each other.

Spring comes, and the grass grows by itself. Love comes, and we act in harmony with all living things to celebrate our love. (Name), today I commit to share my life with you. As we mature as partners, may we always act in full respect of the natural growth development of our love.

(Name), on this, our wedding day, let us each commit to be partner, lover, companion, and, most importantly, friend. The ride may be easy or it may be rough; let us make it together.

I, (name), close one chapter of life and open another today. With you, (name), I commit today to share all that I may be, all that I may become. May each page bear the word of love.

(Name), I ask for nothing more from this good life than that I may live out its days with you. I offer here my hand, my heart, and my soul, and trust utterly they will be safe with you. Let us walk as one.

Whatever lies ahead, good or ill, we will face together. Distance may test us for a time, and time may try us. But if we look to each other first, we will always see a friend. (Name), look to me for all the days to come; today I take my place as your (wife/husband).

Today we take the biggest step of all, and yet a step that comes so easily it hardly seems to need a thought to guide it. My natural place, (name), is by your side. Let me remain there for all my days.

I saw things indistinctly before our love; today all is clear. (Name), I offer myself to you with all certainty. I should be your (husband/wife) and you should be my (husband/wife). Let us become partners today.

A new dawn, a new day, a new life. This is the first of our days together, (name), and each one will be unique. Let us pledge to each other, before this assembly, to receive each day as the invaluable gift it is, and to always face the dawn together.

Now we stand together; may it always be so. (Name), I offer myself to you today as your (husband/wife); I will always love you, respect you, and be faithful to you.

Respecting each other, we commit to live our lives together for all the days to come. (Name), I ask you to share this world with me, for good or for ill. Be my partner, and I will be yours.

A day together begins a lifetime together. (Name), I offer to share with you all that I may encounter, on this day and on all the days that follow.

As steady as the tides, our love has borne me along to this day. (Name), you have changed me. I once was alone; now I am whole only with you. Let us join our lives today and, with our hands joined, face the sun and ride all the waves, gentle and strong, that come our way.

(Name), as long as I have this love, I have my home. Today before these honored guests, I pledge to live my life by your side, forsaking all others.

To understand love means to give without a trace of selfishness. (Name), I know we have built a love that will last, because we have begun to learn to think of we first and I second. Let us continue to learn this lesson for the rest of our lives—and let our marriage be a sign of what love means to all we meet.

Many of the days that have gone before have been celebrations; but this day is different. Many of the days that have gone before have been accompanied by family and friends; but this day is different. Many of the days that have gone before have been marked with the joy of growth and change; but this day is different. Today I join my life to yours, (name). I do so with a certain and happy heart—on a day that marks the beginning of a new life for us.

Because of the joining of man and woman, we all share in this human life. Today we celebrate this renewal of life; today, (name), I join my life with yours, forsaking all others. Let us live and love, not merely for ourselves, but for the entire human family.

Only the beginning—but the beginning of everything in our new role as life-partners. (Name), take this ring as a sign of my love for you and my commitment to this union. This is the beginning—I will be with you until the end.

It is amazing when two people find a real love in this world. It is amazing to watch that love take root and thrive. It is amazing to find yourself in the presence of that love. But when this love has grown strong, (name), as ours has, there is nothing so natural as the decision to commit to that love. I do so here today, and give you all that I am and all that I may become.

The world's storms may storm, and the world's winds may blow, but this love will stay strong. It is today, and will be tomorrow, the center of our lives. (Name), I take you as my (husband/wife) from this day forward. Let us live as one in this world.

Today we move from I to we. (Name), take this ring as a symbol of my decision to join my life with yours until death should part us. I walked to this place to meet you today; we shall walk from it together.

On this day, (month, date, year), I, (name), join myself to you, (name), before this company. May our days be long, and may they be seasoned with love, understanding, and respect.

CHAPTER NINE

Renewing
Your Vows

In this chapter you will find both completed vows that you may use or adapt in a renewal ceremony and a number of quotes that may be appropriate for use in your vows.

Vows to Use or Adapt

Perhaps the only thing truer than one's first true love is to recommit to that love before family and friends. (Name), you were and are my love for life—I take you from this day forward as my (husband/wife).

Today we marry again, and in every moment of every hour of every day that follows, may we continue to join ourselves in marriage. (Name), with love and joy I recommit myself to this marriage, the central fact of my life.

Once before I have stood with you before family and friends; once again I take your hand as my partner. (Name), I take you this day and for all days as my (husband/wife).

I (name), having found the best part of myself in my life with you, (name), today renew the vows of marriage. May we always walk together in peace and understanding.

The word renaissance means "rebirth"; today we celebrate the rebirth of our commitment before this honored gathering. (Name), with full confidence in the solid anchor of our love, I take you once again as my (husband/wife).

The act we perform today, we perform with a solemn understanding of the meaning of our love and our commitment. (Name), take this ring as a sign of my renewed commitment to our life together.

I believe in this marriage more strongly than ever. (Name), it is with joy borne of experience and trust that I commit myself once again to be your (husband/wife).

To continue in joy, love, and friendship is among the greatest gifts God can bestow on his children. (Name), take this ring as a sign of my undying love for you, and continue with me as we make our way in this world.

I, (name), give to you, (name), a new promise, and yet not so new; a new (husband/wife), and yet not so new; and a new affirmation of love from the heart that has loved you for (number) years and will love you for as many more as God allots to it.

Let us share again the promise we made (number) years ago: to honor and cherish one another, to respect, to listen, and above all, to love before all else. (Name), with joy I promise this to you again today, and again give myself to you as your (husband/wife).

Quotes You May Wish to Incorporate into the Ceremony

> Love at first sight is easy to understand; it's when two people have been looking at each other for a lifetime that it becomes a miracle.
>
> **—Sam Levenson**

> Love can never grow old. Locks may lose their brown and gold. Cheeks may fade and hollow grow. But the hearts that love will know, never winter's frost and chill, summer's warmth is in them still.
>
> **—Leo Buscaglia**

Nothing is more beautiful than the love that has weathered the storms of life. The love of the young for the young, that is the beginning of life. But the love of the old for the old, that is the beginning of things longer.

—Jerome K. Jerome

Young love is a flame; very pretty, often very hot and fierce, but still only light and flickering. The love of the older and disciplined heart is as coals, deep burning, unquenchable.

—Henry Ward Beecher

True love is night jasmine, a diamond in darkness, the heartbeat no cardiologist has ever heard. It is the most common of miracles, fashioned of fleecy clouds —a handful of stars tossed into the night sky.

—Jim Bishop

I love you not only for what you have made of yourself, but for what you are making of me.

—Roy Croft

Love is an act of endless forgiveness, a tender look which becomes a habit.

—Peter Ustinov

Love cures people, the ones who receive love and the ones who give it, too.

—Karl A. Menninger

The bonds of marriage are like any other bonds—they mature slowly.

—Peter de Vries

A successful marriage is an edifice that must be rebuilt every day.

—Andre Maurois

Marriage is that relationship between man and woman in which the independence is equal, the dependence mutual, and the obligation reciprocal.

—L. K. Anspacher

The union of souls will ever be more perfect than that of bodies.

—Erasmus

O lay thy hand in mine dear! We're growing old; But Time hath brought no sign, dear, That hearts grow cold. 'Tis long, long since our new love Made life divine; But age enricheth true love, Like noble wine.

—Gerald Massey

Thrice joyous are those united by an unbroken band of love, unsundered by any division before life's final day.

—Horace

But happy they, the happiest of their kind, Whom gentler stars unite, and in one fate
Their hearts, their fortunes, and their beings blend.

—James Thomson

The family is one of nature's masterpieces.

—George Santayana

Unity, to be real, must stand the severest strain without breaking.

—Mahatma Gandhi

And Finally . . .

We offer the following poem, a moving tribute from a husband to a wife during a ceremony renewing wedding vows. Whether used in its entirety or excerpted, this can make for a particularly touching moment during the ceremony.

The Worn Wedding Ring

Your wedding-ring wears thin, dear wife; ah, summers not a few. Since I put it on your finger first, have passed o'er me and you; And, love, what changes we have seen, what cares and pleasures, too Since, you became my own dear wife, when this old ring was new!

O, blessings on that happy day, the happiest of my life, When, thanks to God, your low, sweet "Yes" made you my loving wife! Your heart will say the same, I know; that day's as dear to you, That day that made me yours, dear wife, when this old ring was new.

How well do I remember now your young sweet face that day! How fair you were, how dear you were, my tongue could hardly say; Nor how I doted on you: O, how proud I was of you! But did I love you more than now, when this old ring was new?

No, no! no fairer were you then than at this hour to me; And, dear as life to me this day, how could you dearer be? As sweet your face might be that day as now it is, tis true; But did I know your heart as well when this old ring was new?

O partner of my gladness, wife, what care, what grief is there For me you would not bravely face, with me you would not share? O, what a weary want had every day, if wanting you, Wanting the love that God made mine when this old ring was new!

Years bring fresh links to bind us, wide, young voices that are here; Young faces round our fire that make their mother's yet more dear; Young loving hearts your care each day makes yet more like to you, More like the loving heart made mine when this old ring was new.

And blessed be God! all He has given are with us yet; around Our table every precious life lent to us still is found. Though cares we've known, with hopeful hearts the worst we've struggled through; Blessed be His name for all his love since this old ring was new!

The past is dear; its sweetness still our memories treasure yet; The griefs we've borne, together borne, we would not now forget. Whatever, wife, the future brings, heart unto heart still true, We'll share as we have shared all else since this old ring was new.

And if God spare us 'mongst our sons and daughters to grow old, We know his goodness will not let your heart or mine grow cold. Your aged eyes will see in mine all they've still shown to you. And mine and yours all they have seen since this old ring was new!

And O, when death shall come at last to bid me to my rest, May I die looking in those eyes, and resting on that breast; O, may my parting gaze be blessed with the dear sight of you, Of those fond eyes, fond as they were when this old ring was new.

—William Cox Bennett

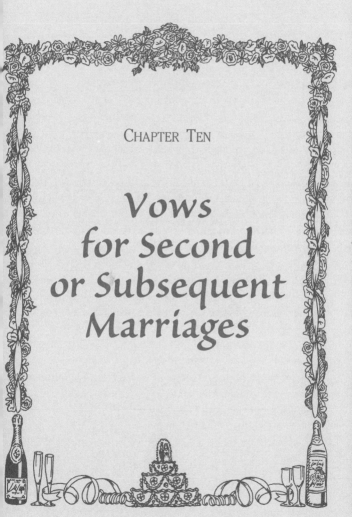

CHAPTER TEN

Vows
for Second
or Subsequent
Marriages

*T*here follow a number of vows designed specifically for ceremonies in which one or both partners are marrying for the second or for a subsequent time. (Of course, you may certainly feel free to adapt one of the vows in earlier chapters to your ceremony as you see fit.) After the vows, you will find a number of quotes you may wish to incorporate into the celebration, either as part of your vow or elsewhere in the proceedings.

Vows to Use or Adapt

We come here as two people who know who we are; neither of us could be who we are today, or could offer to share who we will become tomorrow, without having lived the lives we lived yesterday. (Name), I enter into this marriage with you as an equal partner, secure in the knowledge that we will face our days together with mutual respect. Let us always be willing to grow, to continue to become the people we were meant to be.

I will be your (husband/wife), (name). I will accept you as an independent and equal partner; I will listen to you always; I will respect you and honor you. I am filled with joy that we have found each other.

Since I have found you, (name), I have found a new life. The decision to commit to share that life with you is one I make happily and with full confidence in our love. (Name), let us be husband and wife.

Today we look to the future. (Name), I enter into this marriage with joy and with a firm sense of the importance of sharing our lives as husband and wife. Let us always respect and care for one another from this day forward.

Love is not an end result, but a direction. (Name), I offer myself to you as your (husband/wife) because I know that we should make the journey of life together. Let us never fail to speak honestly, to respect each other, and to work to keep ourselves always on a steady course.

(Name), we enter today on a new and unparalleled journey. As your (husband/wife), I will always listen, always respect you, and always work to help us become the best people we can be. Take this ring as a sign of my love for you.

I take you today as my (husband/wife), (name), because it is when I am with you that I feel most complete. Let us join our lives from this day forward.

(Name), that I join my life with yours today in complete certainty of heart is the joy of my life. Let us be husband and wife.

I, (name), offer myself to you, (name), as your (husband/wife). May we never stop looking to the future, and may we always make time for the present.

(Name), I rejoice today in our decision to join our lives. Today, I take my place beside you as your (husband/wife).

Quotes You May Wish to Incorporate into the Ceremony

Happiness is not a reward—it is a consequence.
—Robert Green Ingersoll

By harmony our souls are swayed; By harmony the world was made.
—George Granville

Life belongs to the living, and he who lives must be
prepared for changes.

—Johann Wolfgang von Goethe

Happiness is the legal tender of the soul.

—Robert G. Ingersoll

In every part and corner of our life, to lose oneself
is to be gainer; to forget oneself is to be happy.

—Robert Louis Stevenson

Oh love, love while love lives.

—Ferdinand Freiligrath

They alone are wise who know how to love.

—Seneca

What we frankly give, forever is our own.

—George Granville

Love is a circle, that doth restless move
In the same sweet eternity of love.

—Robert Herrick

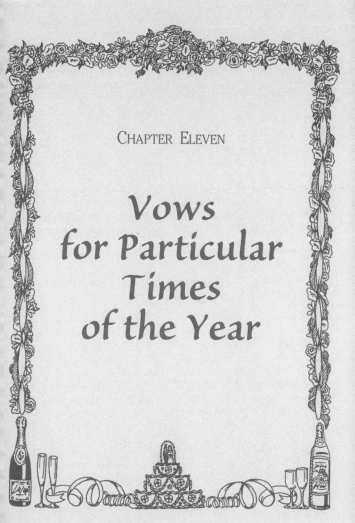

CHAPTER ELEVEN

Vows for Particular Times of the Year

*I*n this part of the book, you'll find a customized vow for each month of the year. Whether you use the vow as written or adapt it to your own tastes, of course, is up to you!

January

A new year, a new commitment, and a new chapter in our lives. (Name), I offer myself to you as your (husband/wife), and I pledge to you that I will strive to keep our marriage rooted in the sense of wonder, newness, and uniqueness that we share today in this honored gathering.

February

(Name), we commit ourselves to each other in a time of winter, but the love that brings us here today is the warmest thing I have ever known in my life. I give myself to you as your (husband/wife) from this day forward.

March

Bride: Initially, March was the first month of the year, because it was the first month in which signs of new growth were visible after the ravages of winter.
Groom: Today we begin our own new spring together.
Bride: From this day forward, (name), March (date) will mark our new beginning—the first day of our life together as a married couple. On this day, and before these witnesses, I give myself to you as your wife.
Groom: From this day forward, (name), March (date) will mark our new beginning—the first day of our life together as a married couple. On this

day, and before these witnesses, I give
myself to you as your husband.

April

With spring comes rebirth, and with this
ceremony we celebrate our new life together.
(Name), I take you as my (husband/wife) and
vow to honor always the ever-renewing force of life that is
the source of our love.

May

The month of May is traditionally a time of dancing, love,
and rejoicing. (Name), I rejoice today with friends and
family as I offer myself to you for the rest of my days as
your (husband/wife).

June

Bride: Some say June was named to honor Juno, the
goddess of marriage and fertility.
Groom: In her honor, the Romans held a festival on the
first day of this enchanting month.
Bride: On this June day, before this honored assembly,
(name), I give myself to you as your wife. May our days
be many and joyous.
Groom: On this June day, before this honored assembly,
(name), I give myself to you as your husband. May our
days be many and joyous.

July

Now, with summer full in its glory, we join hands and
take up our new roles as husband and wife. (Name), I

promise to love and be true to you from this day forward. May our love be as warm and as enduring as the sweetest day of summer.

August

Groom: The poet Edmund Spenser described the month of August as richly arrayed, in garments all of gold.
Bride: Today we formalize and celebrate our union in the company of our friends and family, all of us arrayed in garments befitting the joyous occasion of love confirmed.
Groom: (Name), today I offer myself to you as your husband, forsaking all others, and sure of the power of a love as rare as gold and as rich as the fullest day of summer. I will stand by your side forever.
Bride: (Name), today I offer myself to you as your wife, forsaking all others, and sure of the power of a love as rare as gold and as rich as the fullest day of summer. I will stand by your side forever.

September

Today, on the (number) day of the harvest month of September, we reap the bounty of our love, beginning our life together as husband and wife. (Name), I give myself to you as your partner from this day forward, with thanks and with joy as we prepare to share in all the days of love to come.

October

The leaves change and the seasons turn, but our love is constant. (Name), I join my life with yours on this day and for all the days to come. You are the one with whom I choose to spend all the seasons of my life.

November

Today we join our lives by entering formally into the union of marriage. We are thankful indeed to participate in this sacred rite. (Name), I count it as the chief joy of my life on this earth to offer myself to you today as your (husband/wife).

December

(Name), it is right and fitting that we join as marriage partners at this special time of the year, in the presence of this beloved family and honored friends. I offer myself to you as your (husband/wife); from this day forward, we two shall stand together as one.

The Last Word

By this point, we hope you have enough ideas to develop your own wedding vows—or are comfortable using one of the ones included in this book. At this stage, there remain only two more tasks for us.

The first is to remind you once again to check with your officiant on the requirements of your ceremony. There's no point in falling in love with a particular vow, only to find that it won't be allowed within your tradition. Don't save this task for later—you may be in for an unpleasant surprise if your vow does not conform to the requirements of the ceremony in which you'll be participating.

Second, we want to congratulate you on your upcoming wedding—and wish you and your partner all the best in the years ahead!

Index